Burger

Log Book

THIS BOOK BELONGS TO:

BURGER LOGBOOK

DATE	
BURGER JOINT	SMASH BRO
LOCATION	WARE

		COST	$

BURGER STYLE	SMASHED

TOPPINGS	
✓ LETTUCE	✓ ONION
○ BACON	○ PICKLES
○ TOMATO	✓ CHEESE
○ EGG	○ CHILI
○ AVOCADO	○ MUSHROOMS
○ CHILES	○ OTHER

CONDIMENTS	
✓ KETCHUP	○ MUSTARD
○ THOUSAND ISLAND	✓ MAYONNAISE
○ RANCH	○ RELISH
○ BBQ SAUCE	○ OTHER

TYPE OF BEEF
STEAK

TYPE OF BUN
BRIOCHE

COOKED	
○ PAN-FRIED	✓ SMASHED BURGER
○ STEAMED	○ BROILED
○ CHAR-GRILLED	○ OTHER

SIDES	
○ FRENCH FRIES	○ ZUCCHINI FRIES
○ ONION RINGS	○ SWEET POTATO FRIES
○ SIDE SALAD	○ OTHER

NOTES
Delicious

WOULD YOU GO BACK?		OVERALL RATING
✓ YES	○ NO	9 / 10

BURGER LOGBOOK

DATE	
BURGER JOINT	

LOCATION		COST	$

BURGER STYLE	

TOPPINGS

○ LETTUCE	○ ONION
○ BACON	○ PICKLES
○ TOMATO	○ CHEESE
○ EGG	○ CHILI
○ AVOCADO	○ MUSHROOMS
○ CHILES	○ OTHER

CONDIMENTS

○ KETCHUP	○ MUSTARD
○ THOUSAND ISLAND	○ MAYONNAISE
○ RANCH	○ RELISH
○ BBQ SAUCE	○ OTHER

TYPE OF BEEF

TYPE OF BUN

COOKED

○ PAN-FRIED	○ SMASHED BURGER
○ STEAMED	○ BROILED
○ CHAR-GRILLED	○ OTHER

SIDES

○ FRENCH FRIES	○ ZUCCHINI FRIES
○ ONION RINGS	○ SWEET POTATO FRIES
○ SIDE SALAD	○ OTHER

NOTES

WOULD YOU GO BACK?		OVERALL RATING
○ YES	○ NO	/ 10

BURGER LOGBOOK

DATE	
BURGER JOINT	
LOCATION	COST $
BURGER STYLE	

TOPPINGS	
○ LETTUCE	○ ONION
○ BACON	○ PICKLES
○ TOMATO	○ CHEESE
○ EGG	○ CHILI
○ AVOCADO	○ MUSHROOMS
○ CHILES	○ OTHER

CONDIMENTS	
○ KETCHUP	○ MUSTARD
○ THOUSAND ISLAND	○ MAYONNAISE
○ RANCH	○ RELISH
○ BBQ SAUCE	○ OTHER

TYPE OF BEEF

TYPE OF BUN

COOKED	
○ PAN-FRIED	○ SMASHED BURGER
○ STEAMED	○ BROILED
○ CHAR-GRILLED	○ OTHER

SIDES	
○ FRENCH FRIES	○ ZUCCHINI FRIES
○ ONION RINGS	○ SWEET POTATO FRIES
○ SIDE SALAD	○ OTHER

NOTES

WOULD YOU GO BACK?		OVERALL RATING
○ YES	○ NO	/ 10

BURGER LOGBOOK

DATE	
BURGER JOINT	
LOCATION	COST $
BURGER STYLE	

TOPPINGS

○ LETTUCE	○ ONION
○ BACON	○ PICKLES
○ TOMATO	○ CHEESE
○ EGG	○ CHILI
○ AVOCADO	○ MUSHROOMS
○ CHILES	○ OTHER

CONDIMENTS

○ KETCHUP	○ MUSTARD
○ THOUSAND ISLAND	○ MAYONNAISE
○ RANCH	○ RELISH
○ BBQ SAUCE	○ OTHER

TYPE OF BEEF

TYPE OF BUN

COOKED

○ PAN-FRIED	○ SMASHED BURGER
○ STEAMED	○ BROILED
○ CHAR-GRILLED	○ OTHER

SIDES

○ FRENCH FRIES	○ ZUCCHINI FRIES
○ ONION RINGS	○ SWEET POTATO FRIES
○ SIDE SALAD	○ OTHER

NOTES

WOULD YOU GO BACK?		OVERALL RATING
○ YES	○ NO	/ 10

BURGER LOGBOOK

DATE	
BURGER JOINT	
LOCATION	COST $
BURGER STYLE	

TOPPINGS

○ LETTUCE	○ ONION
○ BACON	○ PICKLES
○ TOMATO	○ CHEESE
○ EGG	○ CHILI
○ AVOCADO	○ MUSHROOMS
○ CHILES	○ OTHER

CONDIMENTS

○ KETCHUP	○ MUSTARD
○ THOUSAND ISLAND	○ MAYONNAISE
○ RANCH	○ RELISH
○ BBQ SAUCE	○ OTHER

TYPE OF BEEF

TYPE OF BUN

COOKED

○ PAN-FRIED	○ SMASHED BURGER
○ STEAMED	○ BROILED
○ CHAR-GRILLED	○ OTHER

SIDES

○ FRENCH FRIES	○ ZUCCHINI FRIES
○ ONION RINGS	○ SWEET POTATO FRIES
○ SIDE SALAD	○ OTHER

NOTES

WOULD YOU GO BACK?		OVERALL RATING
○ YES	○ NO	/ 10

BURGER LOGBOOK

DATE			
BURGER JOINT			
LOCATION		COST	$
BURGER STYLE			

TOPPINGS		TYPE OF BEEF	
○ LETTUCE	○ ONION		
○ BACON	○ PICKLES	**TYPE OF BUN**	
○ TOMATO	○ CHEESE		
○ EGG	○ CHILI	**COOKED**	
○ AVOCADO	○ MUSHROOMS	○ PAN-FRIED	○ SMASHED BURGER
○ CHILES	○ OTHER	○ STEAMED	○ BROILED

CONDIMENTS		○ CHAR-GRILLED	○ OTHER
○ KETCHUP	○ MUSTARD	**SIDES**	
○ THOUSAND ISLAND	○ MAYONNAISE	○ FRENCH FRIES	○ ZUCCHINI FRIES
○ RANCH	○ RELISH	○ ONION RINGS	○ SWEET POTATO FRIES
○ BBQ SAUCE	○ OTHER	○ SIDE SALAD	○ OTHER

NOTES

WOULD YOU GO BACK?		OVERALL RATING
○ YES	○ NO	/ 10

BURGER LOGBOOK

DATE	
BURGER JOINT	

LOCATION		COST	$

BURGER STYLE	

TOPPINGS		TYPE OF BEEF	
○ LETTUCE	○ ONION		
○ BACON	○ PICKLES	**TYPE OF BUN**	
○ TOMATO	○ CHEESE		
○ EGG	○ CHILI	**COOKED**	
○ AVOCADO	○ MUSHROOMS	○ PAN-FRIED	○ SMASHED BURGER
○ CHILES	○ OTHER	○ STEAMED	○ BROILED

CONDIMENTS

		○ CHAR-GRILLED	○ OTHER
○ KETCHUP	○ MUSTARD	**SIDES**	
○ THOUSAND ISLAND	○ MAYONNAISE	○ FRENCH FRIES	○ ZUCCHINI FRIES
○ RANCH	○ RELISH	○ ONION RINGS	○ SWEET POTATO FRIES
○ BBQ SAUCE	○ OTHER	○ SIDE SALAD	○ OTHER

NOTES

WOULD YOU GO BACK?		OVERALL RATING
○ YES	○ NO	/ 10

BURGER LOGBOOK

DATE			
BURGER JOINT			
LOCATION		COST	$
BURGER STYLE			

TOPPINGS		TYPE OF BEEF	
○ LETTUCE	○ ONION		
○ BACON	○ PICKLES	**TYPE OF BUN**	
○ TOMATO	○ CHEESE		
○ EGG	○ CHILI	**COOKED**	
○ AVOCADO	○ MUSHROOMS	○ PAN-FRIED	○ SMASHED BURGER
○ CHILES	○ OTHER	○ STEAMED	○ BROILED
		○ CHAR-GRILLED	○ OTHER

CONDIMENTS		SIDES	
○ KETCHUP	○ MUSTARD		
○ THOUSAND ISLAND	○ MAYONNAISE	○ FRENCH FRIES	○ ZUCCHINI FRIES
○ RANCH	○ RELISH	○ ONION RINGS	○ SWEET POTATO FRIES
○ BBQ SAUCE	○ OTHER	○ SIDE SALAD	○ OTHER

NOTES

WOULD YOU GO BACK?		OVERALL RATING
○ YES	○ NO	/ 10

BURGER LOGBOOK

DATE	
BURGER JOINT	
LOCATION	COST $
BURGER STYLE	

TOPPINGS	
○ LETTUCE	○ ONION
○ BACON	○ PICKLES
○ TOMATO	○ CHEESE
○ EGG	○ CHILI
○ AVOCADO	○ MUSHROOMS
○ CHILES	○ OTHER

CONDIMENTS	
○ KETCHUP	○ MUSTARD
○ THOUSAND ISLAND	○ MAYONNAISE
○ RANCH	○ RELISH
○ BBQ SAUCE	○ OTHER

TYPE OF BEEF

TYPE OF BUN

COOKED	
○ PAN-FRIED	○ SMASHED BURGER
○ STEAMED	○ BROILED
○ CHAR-GRILLED	○ OTHER

SIDES	
○ FRENCH FRIES	○ ZUCCHINI FRIES
○ ONION RINGS	○ SWEET POTATO FRIES
○ SIDE SALAD	○ OTHER

NOTES

WOULD YOU GO BACK?		OVERALL RATING
○ YES	○ NO	/ 10

BURGER LOGBOOK

DATE	
BURGER JOINT	
LOCATION	COST $
BURGER STYLE	

TOPPINGS	
○ LETTUCE	○ ONION
○ BACON	○ PICKLES
○ TOMATO	○ CHEESE
○ EGG	○ CHILI
○ AVOCADO	○ MUSHROOMS
○ CHILES	○ OTHER

CONDIMENTS	
○ KETCHUP	○ MUSTARD
○ THOUSAND ISLAND	○ MAYONNAISE
○ RANCH	○ RELISH
○ BBQ SAUCE	○ OTHER

TYPE OF BEEF

TYPE OF BUN

COOKED	
○ PAN-FRIED	○ SMASHED BURGER
○ STEAMED	○ BROILED
○ CHAR-GRILLED	○ OTHER

SIDES	
○ FRENCH FRIES	○ ZUCCHINI FRIES
○ ONION RINGS	○ SWEET POTATO FRIES
○ SIDE SALAD	○ OTHER

NOTES

WOULD YOU GO BACK?		OVERALL RATING
○ YES	○ NO	/ 10

BURGER LOGBOOK

DATE	
BURGER JOINT	
LOCATION	COST $
BURGER STYLE	

TOPPINGS		TYPE OF BEEF	
○ LETTUCE	○ ONION		
○ BACON	○ PICKLES	**TYPE OF BUN**	
○ TOMATO	○ CHEESE		
○ EGG	○ CHILI	**COOKED**	
○ AVOCADO	○ MUSHROOMS	○ PAN-FRIED	○ SMASHED BURGER
○ CHILES	○ OTHER	○ STEAMED	○ BROILED
		○ CHAR-GRILLED	○ OTHER

CONDIMENTS		SIDES	
○ KETCHUP	○ MUSTARD	○ FRENCH FRIES	○ ZUCCHINI FRIES
○ THOUSAND ISLAND	○ MAYONNAISE	○ ONION RINGS	○ SWEET POTATO FRIES
○ RANCH	○ RELISH	○ SIDE SALAD	○ OTHER
○ BBQ SAUCE	○ OTHER		

NOTES

WOULD YOU GO BACK?		OVERALL RATING
○ YES	○ NO	/ 10

BURGER LOGBOOK

DATE	
BURGER JOINT	
LOCATION	COST $
BURGER STYLE	

TOPPINGS	
○ LETTUCE	○ ONION
○ BACON	○ PICKLES
○ TOMATO	○ CHEESE
○ EGG	○ CHILI
○ AVOCADO	○ MUSHROOMS
○ CHILES	○ OTHER

CONDIMENTS	
○ KETCHUP	○ MUSTARD
○ THOUSAND ISLAND	○ MAYONNAISE
○ RANCH	○ RELISH
○ BBQ SAUCE	○ OTHER

TYPE OF BEEF

TYPE OF BUN

COOKED	
○ PAN-FRIED	○ SMASHED BURGER
○ STEAMED	○ BROILED
○ CHAR-GRILLED	○ OTHER

SIDES	
○ FRENCH FRIES	○ ZUCCHINI FRIES
○ ONION RINGS	○ SWEET POTATO FRIES
○ SIDE SALAD	○ OTHER

NOTES

WOULD YOU GO BACK?		OVERALL RATING
○ YES	○ NO	/ 10

BURGER LOGBOOK

DATE	
BURGER JOINT	
LOCATION	COST $
BURGER STYLE	

TOPPINGS

○ LETTUCE	○ ONION
○ BACON	○ PICKLES
○ TOMATO	○ CHEESE
○ EGG	○ CHILI
○ AVOCADO	○ MUSHROOMS
○ CHILES	○ OTHER

CONDIMENTS

○ KETCHUP	○ MUSTARD
○ THOUSAND ISLAND	○ MAYONNAISE
○ RANCH	○ RELISH
○ BBQ SAUCE	○ OTHER

TYPE OF BEEF

TYPE OF BUN

COOKED

○ PAN-FRIED	○ SMASHED BURGER
○ STEAMED	○ BROILED
○ CHAR-GRILLED	○ OTHER

SIDES

○ FRENCH FRIES	○ ZUCCHINI FRIES
○ ONION RINGS	○ SWEET POTATO FRIES
○ SIDE SALAD	○ OTHER

NOTES

WOULD YOU GO BACK?		OVERALL RATING
○ YES	○ NO	/ 10

BURGER LOGBOOK

DATE	
BURGER JOINT	
LOCATION	COST $
BURGER STYLE	

TOPPINGS		TYPE OF BEEF	
○ LETTUCE	○ ONION		
○ BACON	○ PICKLES	**TYPE OF BUN**	
○ TOMATO	○ CHEESE		
○ EGG	○ CHILI	**COOKED**	
○ AVOCADO	○ MUSHROOMS	○ PAN-FRIED	○ SMASHED BURGER
○ CHILES	○ OTHER	○ STEAMED	○ BROILED
		○ CHAR-GRILLED	○ OTHER

CONDIMENTS		SIDES	
○ KETCHUP	○ MUSTARD		
○ THOUSAND ISLAND	○ MAYONNAISE	○ FRENCH FRIES	○ ZUCCHINI FRIES
○ RANCH	○ RELISH	○ ONION RINGS	○ SWEET POTATO FRIES
○ BBQ SAUCE	○ OTHER	○ SIDE SALAD	○ OTHER

NOTES

WOULD YOU GO BACK?		OVERALL RATING
○ YES	○ NO	/ 10

BURGER LOGBOOK

DATE	
BURGER JOINT	
LOCATION	COST $
BURGER STYLE	

TOPPINGS

○ LETTUCE	○ ONION
○ BACON	○ PICKLES
○ TOMATO	○ CHEESE
○ EGG	○ CHILI
○ AVOCADO	○ MUSHROOMS
○ CHILES	○ OTHER

CONDIMENTS

○ KETCHUP	○ MUSTARD
○ THOUSAND ISLAND	○ MAYONNAISE
○ RANCH	○ RELISH
○ BBQ SAUCE	○ OTHER

TYPE OF BEEF

TYPE OF BUN

COOKED

○ PAN-FRIED	○ SMASHED BURGER
○ STEAMED	○ BROILED
○ CHAR-GRILLED	○ OTHER

SIDES

○ FRENCH FRIES	○ ZUCCHINI FRIES
○ ONION RINGS	○ SWEET POTATO FRIES
○ SIDE SALAD	○ OTHER

NOTES

WOULD YOU GO BACK?		OVERALL RATING
○ YES	○ NO	/ 10

BURGER LOGBOOK

DATE	
BURGER JOINT	
LOCATION	COST $
BURGER STYLE	

TOPPINGS		TYPE OF BEEF	
○ LETTUCE	○ ONION		
○ BACON	○ PICKLES	**TYPE OF BUN**	
○ TOMATO	○ CHEESE		
○ EGG	○ CHILI	**COOKED**	
○ AVOCADO	○ MUSHROOMS	○ PAN-FRIED	○ SMASHED BURGER
○ CHILES	○ OTHER	○ STEAMED	○ BROILED

CONDIMENTS		○ CHAR-GRILLED	○ OTHER
○ KETCHUP	○ MUSTARD	**SIDES**	
○ THOUSAND ISLAND	○ MAYONNAISE	○ FRENCH FRIES	○ ZUCCHINI FRIES
○ RANCH	○ RELISH	○ ONION RINGS	○ SWEET POTATO FRIES
○ BBQ SAUCE	○ OTHER	○ SIDE SALAD	○ OTHER

NOTES

WOULD YOU GO BACK?		OVERALL RATING
○ YES	○ NO	/ 10

BURGER LOGBOOK

DATE	
BURGER JOINT	
LOCATION	COST $
BURGER STYLE	

TOPPINGS

○ LETTUCE	○ ONION
○ BACON	○ PICKLES
○ TOMATO	○ CHEESE
○ EGG	○ CHILI
○ AVOCADO	○ MUSHROOMS
○ CHILES	○ OTHER

CONDIMENTS

○ KETCHUP	○ MUSTARD
○ THOUSAND ISLAND	○ MAYONNAISE
○ RANCH	○ RELISH
○ BBQ SAUCE	○ OTHER

TYPE OF BEEF

TYPE OF BUN

COOKED

○ PAN-FRIED	○ SMASHED BURGER
○ STEAMED	○ BROILED
○ CHAR-GRILLED	○ OTHER

SIDES

○ FRENCH FRIES	○ ZUCCHINI FRIES
○ ONION RINGS	○ SWEET POTATO FRIES
○ SIDE SALAD	○ OTHER

NOTES

WOULD YOU GO BACK?		OVERALL RATING
○ YES	○ NO	/ 10

BURGER LOGBOOK

DATE	
BURGER JOINT	
LOCATION	COST $
BURGER STYLE	

TOPPINGS	
○ LETTUCE	○ ONION
○ BACON	○ PICKLES
○ TOMATO	○ CHEESE
○ EGG	○ CHILI
○ AVOCADO	○ MUSHROOMS
○ CHILES	○ OTHER

CONDIMENTS	
○ KETCHUP	○ MUSTARD
○ THOUSAND ISLAND	○ MAYONNAISE
○ RANCH	○ RELISH
○ BBQ SAUCE	○ OTHER

TYPE OF BEEF

TYPE OF BUN

COOKED	
○ PAN-FRIED	○ SMASHED BURGER
○ STEAMED	○ BROILED
○ CHAR-GRILLED	○ OTHER

SIDES	
○ FRENCH FRIES	○ ZUCCHINI FRIES
○ ONION RINGS	○ SWEET POTATO FRIES
○ SIDE SALAD	○ OTHER

NOTES

WOULD YOU GO BACK?		OVERALL RATING
○ YES	○ NO	/ 10

BURGER LOGBOOK

DATE	
BURGER JOINT	
LOCATION	COST $
BURGER STYLE	

TOPPINGS

○ LETTUCE	○ ONION
○ BACON	○ PICKLES
○ TOMATO	○ CHEESE
○ EGG	○ CHILI
○ AVOCADO	○ MUSHROOMS
○ CHILES	○ OTHER

CONDIMENTS

○ KETCHUP	○ MUSTARD
○ THOUSAND ISLAND	○ MAYONNAISE
○ RANCH	○ RELISH
○ BBQ SAUCE	○ OTHER

TYPE OF BEEF

TYPE OF BUN

COOKED

○ PAN-FRIED	○ SMASHED BURGER
○ STEAMED	○ BROILED
○ CHAR-GRILLED	○ OTHER

SIDES

○ FRENCH FRIES	○ ZUCCHINI FRIES
○ ONION RINGS	○ SWEET POTATO FRIES
○ SIDE SALAD	○ OTHER

NOTES

WOULD YOU GO BACK?		OVERALL RATING
○ YES	○ NO	/ 10

BURGER LOGBOOK

DATE	
BURGER JOINT	

LOCATION		COST	$

BURGER STYLE	

TOPPINGS

○ LETTUCE	○ ONION
○ BACON	○ P CKLES
○ TOMATO	○ CHEESE
○ EGG	○ CHILI
○ AVOCADO	○ MUSHROOMS
○ CHILES	○ OTHER

CONDIMENTS

○ KETCHUP	○ MUSTARD
○ THOUSAND ISLAND	○ MAYONNAISE
○ RANCH	○ RELISH
○ BBQ SAUCE	○ OTHER

TYPE OF BEEF

TYPE OF BUN

COOKED

○ PAN-FRIED	○ SMASHED BURGER
○ STEAMED	○ BROILED
○ CHAR-GRILLED	○ OTHER

SIDES

○ FRENCH FRIES	○ ZUCCHINI FRIES
○ ONION RINGS	○ SWEET POTATO FRIES
○ SIDE SALAD	○ OTHER

NOTES

WOULD YOU GO BACK?		OVERALL RATING
○ YES	○ NO	/ 10

BURGER LOGBOOK

DATE	
BURGER JOINT	
LOCATION	COST $
BURGER STYLE	

TOPPINGS	
○ LETTUCE	○ ONION
○ BACON	○ PICKLES
○ TOMATO	○ CHEESE
○ EGG	○ CHILI
○ AVOCADO	○ MUSHROOMS
○ CHILES	○ OTHER

CONDIMENTS	
○ KETCHUP	○ MUSTARD
○ THOUSAND ISLAND	○ MAYONNAISE
○ RANCH	○ RELISH
○ BBQ SAUCE	○ OTHER

TYPE OF BEEF

TYPE OF BUN

COOKED	
○ PAN-FRIED	○ SMASHED BURGER
○ STEAMED	○ BROILED
○ CHAR-GRILLED	○ OTHER

SIDES	
○ FRENCH FRIES	○ ZUCCHINI FRIES
○ ONION RINGS	○ SWEET POTATO FRIES
○ SIDE SALAD	○ OTHER

NOTES

WOULD YOU GO BACK?		OVERALL RATING
○ YES	○ NO	/ 10

BURGER LOGBOOK

DATE	
BURGER JOINT	
LOCATION	COST $
BURGER STYLE	

TOPPINGS

○ LETTUCE	○ ONION
○ BACON	○ PICKLES
○ TOMATO	○ CHEESE
○ EGG	○ CHILI
○ AVOCADO	○ MUSHROOMS
○ CHILES	○ OTHER

CONDIMENTS

○ KETCHUP	○ MUSTARD
○ THOUSAND ISLAND	○ MAYONNAISE
○ RANCH	○ RELISH
○ BBQ SAUCE	○ OTHER

TYPE OF BEEF

TYPE OF BUN

COOKED

○ PAN-FRIED	○ SMASHED BURGER
○ STEAMED	○ BROILED
○ CHAR-GRILLED	○ OTHER

SIDES

○ FRENCH FRIES	○ ZUCCHINI FRIES
○ ONION RINGS	○ SWEET POTATO FRIES
○ SIDE SALAD	○ OTHER

NOTES

WOULD YOU GO BACK?		OVERALL RATING
○ YES	○ NO	/ 10

BURGER LOGBOOK

DATE	
BURGER JOINT	
LOCATION	**COST** $
BURGER STYLE	

TOPPINGS		TYPE OF BEEF
○ LETTUCE	○ ONION	
○ BACON	○ PICKLES	**TYPE OF BUN**
○ TOMATO	○ CHEESE	
○ EGG	○ CHILI	**COOKED**
○ AVOCADO	○ MUSHROOMS	
○ CHILES	○ OTHER	

TOPPINGS

○ LETTUCE	○ ONION
○ BACON	○ PICKLES
○ TOMATO	○ CHEESE
○ EGG	○ CHILI
○ AVOCADO	○ MUSHROOMS
○ CHILES	○ OTHER

CONDIMENTS

○ KETCHUP	○ MUSTARD
○ THOUSAND ISLAND	○ MAYONNAISE
○ RANCH	○ RELISH
○ BBQ SAUCE	○ OTHER

TYPE OF BEEF

TYPE OF BUN

COOKED

○ PAN-FRIED	○ SMASHED BURGER
○ STEAMED	○ BROILED
○ CHAR-GRILLED	○ OTHER

SIDES

○ FRENCH FRIES	○ ZUCCHINI FRIES
○ ONION RINGS	○ SWEET POTATO FRIES
○ SIDE SALAD	○ OTHER

NOTES

WOULD YOU GO BACK?

○ YES	○ NO

OVERALL RATING

/ 10

BURGER LOGBOOK

DATE	
BURGER JOINT	
LOCATION	COST $
BURGER STYLE	

TOPPINGS	
○ LETTUCE	○ ONION
○ BACON	○ PICKLES
○ TOMATO	○ CHEESE
○ EGG	○ CHILI
○ AVOCADO	○ MUSHROOMS
○ CHILES	○ OTHER

CONDIMENTS	
○ KETCHUP	○ MUSTARD
○ THOUSAND ISLAND	○ MAYONNAISE
○ RANCH	○ RELISH
○ BBQ SAUCE	○ OTHER

TYPE OF BEEF

TYPE OF BUN

COOKED	
○ PAN-FRIED	○ SMASHED BURGER
○ STEAMED	○ BROILED
○ CHAR-GRILLED	○ OTHER

SIDES	
○ FRENCH FRIES	○ ZUCCHINI FRIES
○ ONION RINGS	○ SWEET POTATO FRIES
○ SIDE SALAD	○ OTHER

NOTES

WOULD YOU GO BACK?	OVERALL RATING
○ YES ○ NO	/ 10

BURGER LOGBOOK

DATE	
BURGER JOINT	
LOCATION	COST \$
BURGER STYLE	

TOPPINGS

○ LETTUCE	○ ONION
○ BACON	○ PICKLES
○ TOMATO	○ CHEESE
○ EGG	○ CHILI
○ AVOCADO	○ MUSHROOMS
○ CHILES	○ OTHER

CONDIMENTS

○ KETCHUP	○ MUSTARD
○ THOUSAND ISLAND	○ MAYONNAISE
○ RANCH	○ RELISH
○ BBQ SAUCE	○ OTHER

TYPE OF BEEF

TYPE OF BUN

COOKED

○ PAN-FRIED	○ SMASHED BURGER
○ STEAMED	○ BROILED
○ CHAR-GRILLED	○ OTHER

SIDES

○ FRENCH FRIES	○ ZUCCHINI FRIES
○ ONION RINGS	○ SWEET POTATO FRIES
○ SIDE SALAD	○ OTHER

NOTES

WOULD YOU GO BACK?		OVERALL RATING
○ YES	○ NO	/ 10

BURGER LOGBOOK

DATE	
BURGER JOINT	
LOCATION	COST $
BURGER STYLE	

TOPPINGS

○ LETTUCE	○ ONION
○ BACON	○ PICKLES
○ TOMATO	○ CHEESE
○ EGG	○ CHILI
○ AVOCADO	○ MUSHROOMS
○ CHILES	○ OTHER

CONDIMENTS

○ KETCHUP	○ MUSTARD
○ THOUSAND ISLAND	○ MAYONNAISE
○ RANCH	○ RELISH
○ BBQ SAUCE	○ OTHER

TYPE OF BEEF

TYPE OF BUN

COOKED

○ PAN-FRIED	○ SMASHED BURGER
○ STEAMED	○ BROILED
○ CHAR-GRILLED	○ OTHER

SIDES

○ FRENCH FRIES	○ ZUCCHINI FRIES
○ ONION RINGS	○ SWEET POTATO FRIES
○ SIDE SALAD	○ OTHER

NOTES

WOULD YOU GO BACK?		OVERALL RATING
○ YES	○ NO	/ 10

BURGER LOGBOOK

DATE	
BURGER JOINT	
LOCATION	COST $
BURGER STYLE	

TOPPINGS		TYPE OF BEEF	
○ LETTUCE	○ ONION		
○ BACON	○ PICKLES	**TYPE OF BUN**	
○ TOMATO	○ CHEESE		
○ EGG	○ CHILI	**COOKED**	
○ AVOCADO	○ MUSHROOMS	○ PAN-FRIED	○ SMASHED BURGER
○ CHILES	○ OTHER	○ STEAMED	○ BROILED

CONDIMENTS		○ CHAR-GRILLED	○ OTHER
○ KETCHUP	○ MUSTARD	**SIDES**	
○ THOUSAND ISLAND	○ MAYONNAISE	○ FRENCH FRIES	○ ZUCCHINI FRIES
○ RANCH	○ RELISH	○ ONION RINGS	○ SWEET POTATO FRIES
○ BBQ SAUCE	○ OTHER	○ SIDE SALAD	○ OTHER

NOTES

WOULD YOU GO BACK?		OVERALL RATING
○ YES	○ NO	/ 10

BURGER LOGBOOK

DATE			
BURGER JOINT			
LOCATION		COST	$
BURGER STYLE			

TOPPINGS		TYPE OF BEEF	
○ LETTUCE	○ ONION		

TYPE OF BUN

TOPPINGS (cont)		
○ BACON	○ PICKLES	
○ TOMATO	○ CHEESE	

		COOKED	
○ EGG	○ CHILI		
○ AVOCADO	○ MUSHROOMS	○ PAN-FRIED	○ SMASHED BURGER
○ CHILES	○ OTHER	○ STEAMED	○ BROILED
CONDIMENTS		○ CHAR-GRILLED	○ OTHER

CONDIMENTS		SIDES	
○ KETCHUP	○ MUSTARD		
○ THOUSAND ISLAND	○ MAYONNAISE	○ FRENCH FRIES	○ ZUCCHINI FRIES
○ RANCH	○ RELISH	○ ONION RINGS	○ SWEET POTATO FRIES
○ BBQ SAUCE	○ OTHER	○ SIDE SALAD	○ OTHER

NOTES

WOULD YOU GO BACK?		OVERALL RATING
○ YES	○ NO	/ 10

BURGER LOGBOOK

DATE	
BURGER JOINT	
LOCATION	COST $
BURGER STYLE	

TOPPINGS

○ LETTUCE	○ ONION
○ BACON	○ PICKLES
○ TOMATO	○ CHEESE
○ EGG	○ CHILI
○ AVOCADO	○ MUSHROOMS
○ CHILES	○ OTHER

CONDIMENTS

○ KETCHUP	○ MUSTARD
○ THOUSAND ISLAND	○ MAYONNAISE
○ RANCH	○ RELISH
○ BBQ SAUCE	○ OTHER

TYPE OF BEEF

TYPE OF BUN

COOKED

○ PAN-FRIED	○ SMASHED BURGER
○ STEAMED	○ BROILED
○ CHAR-GRILLED	○ OTHER

SIDES

○ FRENCH FRIES	○ ZUCCHINI FRIES
○ ONION RINGS	○ SWEET POTATO FRIES
○ SIDE SALAD	○ OTHER

NOTES

WOULD YOU GO BACK?		OVERALL RATING
○ YES	○ NO	/ 10

BURGER LOGBOOK

DATE	
BURGER JOINT	
LOCATION	COST $
BURGER STYLE	

TOPPINGS

○ LETTUCE	○ ONION
○ BACON	○ PICKLES
○ TOMATO	○ CHEESE
○ EGG	○ CHILI
○ AVOCADO	○ MUSHROOMS
○ CHILES	○ OTHER

CONDIMENTS

○ KETCHUP	○ MUSTARD
○ THOUSAND ISLAND	○ MAYONNAISE
○ RANCH	○ RELISH
○ BBQ SAUCE	○ OTHER

TYPE OF BEEF

TYPE OF BUN

COOKED

○ PAN-FRIED	○ SMASHED BURGER
○ STEAMED	○ BROILED
○ CHAR-GRILLED	○ OTHER

SIDES

○ FRENCH FRIES	○ ZUCCHINI FRIES
○ ONION RINGS	○ SWEET POTATO FRIES
○ SIDE SALAD	○ OTHER

NOTES

WOULD YOU GO BACK?		OVERALL RATING
○ YES	○ NO	/ 10

BURGER LOGBOOK

DATE	
BURGER JOINT	
LOCATION	COST $
BURGER STYLE	

TOPPINGS

○ LETTUCE	○ ONION
○ BACON	○ PICKLES
○ TOMATO	○ CHEESE
○ EGG	○ CHILI
○ AVOCADO	○ MUSHROOMS
○ CHILES	○ OTHER

CONDIMENTS

○ KETCHUP	○ MUSTARD
○ THOUSAND ISLAND	○ MAYONNAISE
○ RANCH	○ RELISH
○ BBQ SAUCE	○ OTHER

TYPE OF BEEF

TYPE OF BUN

COOKED

○ PAN-FRIED	○ SMASHED BURGER
○ STEAMED	○ BROILED
○ CHAR-GRILLED	○ OTHER

SIDES

○ FRENCH FRIES	○ ZUCCHINI FRIES
○ ONION RINGS	○ SWEET POTATO FRIES
○ SIDE SALAD	○ OTHER

NOTES

WOULD YOU GO BACK?

○ YES	○ NO

OVERALL RATING

/ 10

BURGER LOGBOOK

DATE			
BURGER JOINT			
LOCATION		COST	$
BURGER STYLE			

TOPPINGS		TYPE OF BEEF	
○ LETTUCE	○ ONION		
○ BACON	○ P CKLES	**TYPE OF BUN**	
○ TOMATO	○ CHEESE		
○ EGG	○ CHILI	**COOKED**	
○ AVOCADO	○ MUSHROOMS	○ PAN-FRIED	○ SMASHED BURGER
○ CHILES	○ OTHER	○ STEAMED	○ BROILED
CONDIMENTS		○ CHAR-GRILLED	○ OTHER
○ KETCHUP	○ MUSTARD	**SIDES**	
○ THOUSAND ISLAND	○ MAYONNAISE	○ FRENCH FRIES	○ ZUCCHINI FRIES
○ RANCH	○ RELISH	○ ONION RINGS	○ SWEET POTATO FRIES
○ BBQ SAUCE	○ OTHER	○ SIDE SALAD	○ OTHER

NOTES

WOULD YOU GO BACK?		OVERALL RATING
○ YES	○ NO	/ 10

BURGER LOGBOOK

DATE	
BURGER JOINT	
LOCATION	COST $
BURGER STYLE	

TOPPINGS	
○ LETTUCE	○ ONION
○ BACON	○ PICKLES
○ TOMATO	○ CHEESE
○ EGG	○ CHILI
○ AVOCADO	○ MUSHROOMS
○ CHILES	○ OTHER

CONDIMENTS	
○ KETCHUP	○ MUSTARD
○ THOUSAND ISLAND	○ MAYONNAISE
○ RANCH	○ RELISH
○ BBQ SAUCE	○ OTHER

TYPE OF BEEF

TYPE OF BUN

COOKED	
○ PAN-FRIED	○ SMASHED BURGER
○ STEAMED	○ BROILED
○ CHAR-GRILLED	○ OTHER

SIDES	
○ FRENCH FRIES	○ ZUCCHINI FRIES
○ ONION RINGS	○ SWEET POTATO FRIES
○ SIDE SALAD	○ OTHER

NOTES

WOULD YOU GO BACK?		OVERALL RATING
○ YES	○ NO	/ 10

BURGER LOGBOOK

DATE	
BURGER JOINT	

LOCATION		COST	$

BURGER STYLE	

TOPPINGS

○ LETTUCE	○ ONION
○ BACON	○ PICKLES
○ TOMATO	○ CHEESE
○ EGG	○ CHILI
○ AVOCADO	○ MUSHROOMS
○ CHILES	○ OTHER

CONDIMENTS

○ KETCHUP	○ MUSTARD
○ THOUSAND ISLAND	○ MAYONNAISE
○ RANCH	○ RELISH
○ BBQ SAUCE	○ OTHER

TYPE OF BEEF

TYPE OF BUN

COOKED

○ PAN-FRIED	○ SMASHED BURGER
○ STEAMED	○ BROILED
○ CHAR-GRILLED	○ OTHER

SIDES

○ FRENCH FRIES	○ ZUCCHINI FRIES
○ ONION RINGS	○ SWEET POTATO FRIES
○ SIDE SALAD	○ OTHER

NOTES

WOULD YOU GO BACK?		OVERALL RATING
○ YES	○ NO	/ 10

BURGER LOGBOOK

DATE	
BURGER JOINT	
LOCATION	COST $
BURGER STYLE	

TOPPINGS

○ LETTUCE	○ ONION
○ BACON	○ PICKLES
○ TOMATO	○ CHEESE
○ EGG	○ CHILI
○ AVOCADO	○ MUSHROOMS
○ CHILES	○ OTHER

CONDIMENTS

○ KETCHUP	○ MUSTARD
○ THOUSAND ISLAND	○ MAYONNAISE
○ RANCH	○ RELISH
○ BBQ SAUCE	○ OTHER

TYPE OF BEEF

TYPE OF BUN

COOKED

○ PAN-FRIED	○ SMASHED BURGER
○ STEAMED	○ BROILED
○ CHAR-GRILLED	○ OTHER

SIDES

○ FRENCH FRIES	○ ZUCCHINI FRIES
○ ONION RINGS	○ SWEET POTATO FRIES
○ SIDE SALAD	○ OTHER

NOTES

WOULD YOU GO BACK?

○ YES	○ NO

OVERALL RATING

/ 10

BURGER LOGBOOK

DATE	
BURGER JOINT	
LOCATION	COST $
BURGER STYLE	

TOPPINGS

○ LETTUCE	○ ONION
○ BACON	○ PICKLES
○ TOMATO	○ CHEESE
○ EGG	○ CHILI
○ AVOCADO	○ MUSHROOMS
○ CHILES	○ OTHER

CONDIMENTS

○ KETCHUP	○ MUSTARD
○ THOUSAND ISLAND	○ MAYONNAISE
○ RANCH	○ RELISH
○ BBQ SAUCE	○ OTHER

TYPE OF BEEF

TYPE OF BUN

COOKED

○ PAN-FRIED	○ SMASHED BURGER
○ STEAMED	○ BROILED
○ CHAR-GRILLED	○ OTHER

SIDES

○ FRENCH FRIES	○ ZUCCHINI FRIES
○ ONION RINGS	○ SWEET POTATO FRIES
○ SIDE SALAD	○ OTHER

NOTES

WOULD YOU GO BACK?		OVERALL RATING
○ YES	○ NO	/ 10

BURGER LOGBOOK

DATE	
BURGER JOINT	
LOCATION	COST $
BURGER STYLE	

TOPPINGS

○ LETTUCE	○ ONION
○ BACON	○ PICKLES
○ TOMATO	○ CHEESE
○ EGG	○ CHILI
○ AVOCADO	○ MUSHROOMS
○ CHILES	○ OTHER

CONDIMENTS

○ KETCHUP	○ MUSTARD
○ THOUSAND ISLAND	○ MAYONNAISE
○ RANCH	○ RELISH
○ BBQ SAUCE	○ OTHER

TYPE OF BEEF

TYPE OF BUN

COOKED

○ PAN-FRIED	○ SMASHED BURGER
○ STEAMED	○ BROILED
○ CHAR-GRILLED	○ OTHER

SIDES

○ FRENCH FRIES	○ ZUCCHINI FRIES
○ ONION RINGS	○ SWEET POTATO FRIES
○ SIDE SALAD	○ OTHER

NOTES

WOULD YOU GO BACK?		OVERALL RATING
○ YES	○ NO	/ 10

BURGER LOGBOOK

DATE	
BURGER JOINT	
LOCATION	COST $
BURGER STYLE	

TOPPINGS

○ LETTUCE	○ ONION
○ BACON	○ PICKLES
○ TOMATO	○ CHEESE
○ EGG	○ CHILI
○ AVOCADO	○ MUSHROOMS
○ CHILES	○ OTHER

CONDIMENTS

○ KETCHUP	○ MUSTARD
○ THOUSAND ISLAND	○ MAYONNAISE
○ RANCH	○ RELISH
○ BBQ SAUCE	○ OTHER

TYPE OF BEEF

TYPE OF BUN

COOKED

○ PAN-FRIED	○ SMASHED BURGER
○ STEAMED	○ BROILED
○ CHAR-GRILLED	○ OTHER

SIDES

○ FRENCH FRIES	○ ZUCCHINI FRIES
○ ONION RINGS	○ SWEET POTATO FRIES
○ SIDE SALAD	○ OTHER

NOTES

WOULD YOU GO BACK?		OVERALL RATING
○ YES	○ NO	/ 10

BURGER LOGBOOK

DATE	
BURGER JOINT	
LOCATION	**COST** $
BURGER STYLE	

TOPPINGS		TYPE OF BEEF
○ LETTUCE	○ ONION	
○ BACON	○ PICKLES	**TYPE OF BUN**
○ TOMATO	○ CHEESE	
○ EGG	○ CHILI	**COOKED**
○ AVOCADO	○ MUSHROOMS	○ PAN-FRIED / ○ SMASHED BURGER
○ CHILES	○ OTHER	○ STEAMED / ○ BROILED

TOPPINGS

○ LETTUCE	○ ONION
○ BACON	○ PICKLES
○ TOMATO	○ CHEESE
○ EGG	○ CHILI
○ AVOCADO	○ MUSHROOMS
○ CHILES	○ OTHER

CONDIMENTS

○ KETCHUP	○ MUSTARD
○ THOUSAND ISLAND	○ MAYONNAISE
○ RANCH	○ RELISH
○ BBQ SAUCE	○ OTHER

TYPE OF BEEF

TYPE OF BUN

COOKED

○ PAN-FRIED	○ SMASHED BURGER
○ STEAMED	○ BROILED
○ CHAR-GRILLED	○ OTHER

SIDES

○ FRENCH FRIES	○ ZUCCHINI FRIES
○ ONION RINGS	○ SWEET POTATO FRIES
○ SIDE SALAD	○ OTHER

NOTES

WOULD YOU GO BACK?		OVERALL RATING
○ YES	○ NO	/ 10

BURGER LOGBOOK

DATE			
BURGER JOINT			
LOCATION		COST	$
BURGER STYLE			

TOPPINGS		TYPE OF BEEF	
○ LETTUCE	○ ONION		
○ BACON	○ PICKLES	**TYPE OF BUN**	
○ TOMATO	○ CHEESE		
○ EGG	○ CHILI	**COOKED**	
○ AVOCADO	○ MUSHROOMS	○ PAN-FRIED	○ SMASHED BURGER
○ CHILES	○ OTHER	○ STEAMED	○ BROILED

CONDIMENTS		○ CHAR-GRILLED	○ OTHER
○ KETCHUP	○ MUSTARD	**SIDES**	
○ THOUSAND ISLAND	○ MAYONNAISE	○ FRENCH FRIES	○ ZUCCHINI FRIES
○ RANCH	○ RELISH	○ ONION RINGS	○ SWEET POTATO FRIES
○ BBQ SAUCE	○ OTHER	○ SIDE SALAD	○ OTHER

NOTES

WOULD YOU GO BACK?		OVERALL RATING
○ YES	○ NO	/ 10

BURGER LOGBOOK

DATE	
BURGER JOINT	
LOCATION	COST $
BURGER STYLE	

TOPPINGS

○ LETTUCE	○ ONION
○ BACON	○ PICKLES
○ TOMATO	○ CHEESE
○ EGG	○ CHILI
○ AVOCADO	○ MUSHROOMS
○ CHILES	○ OTHER

CONDIMENTS

○ KETCHUP	○ MUSTARD
○ THOUSAND ISLAND	○ MAYONNAISE
○ RANCH	○ RELISH
○ BBQ SAUCE	○ OTHER

TYPE OF BEEF

TYPE OF BUN

COOKED

○ PAN-FRIED	○ SMASHED BURGER
○ STEAMED	○ BROILED
○ CHAR-GRILLED	○ OTHER

SIDES

○ FRENCH FRIES	○ ZUCCHINI FRIES
○ ONION RINGS	○ SWEET POTATO FRIES
○ SIDE SALAD	○ OTHER

NOTES

WOULD YOU GO BACK?		OVERALL RATING
○ YES	○ NO	/ 10

BURGER LOGBOOK

DATE	
BURGER JOINT	
LOCATION	COST $
BURGER STYLE	

TOPPINGS

○ LETTUCE	○ ONION
○ BACON	○ PICKLES
○ TOMATO	○ CHEESE
○ EGG	○ CHILI
○ AVOCADO	○ MUSHROOMS
○ CHILES	○ OTHER

CONDIMENTS

○ KETCHUP	○ MUSTARD
○ THOUSAND ISLAND	○ MAYONNAISE
○ RANCH	○ RELISH
○ BBQ SAUCE	○ OTHER

TYPE OF BEEF

TYPE OF BUN

COOKED

○ PAN-FRIED	○ SMASHED BURGER
○ STEAMED	○ BROILED
○ CHAR-GRILLED	○ OTHER

SIDES

○ FRENCH FRIES	○ ZUCCHINI FRIES
○ ONION RINGS	○ SWEET POTATO FRIES
○ SIDE SALAD	○ OTHER

NOTES

WOULD YOU GO BACK?		OVERALL RATING
○ YES	○ NO	/ 10

BURGER LOGBOOK

DATE			
BURGER JOINT			
LOCATION		COST	$
BURGER STYLE			

TOPPINGS		TYPE OF BEEF	
○ LETTUCE	○ ONION		
○ BACON	○ PICKLES	**TYPE OF BUN**	
○ TOMATO	○ CHEESE		
○ EGG	○ CHILI	**COOKED**	
○ AVOCADO	○ MUSHROOMS	○ PAN-FRIED	○ SMASHED BURGER
○ CHILES	○ OTHER	○ STEAMED	○ BROILED

CONDIMENTS		○ CHAR-GRILLED	○ OTHER
○ KETCHUP	○ MUSTARD	**SIDES**	
○ THOUSAND ISLAND	○ MAYONNAISE	○ FRENCH FRIES	○ ZUCCHINI FRIES
○ RANCH	○ RELISH	○ ONION RINGS	○ SWEET POTATO FRIES
○ BBQ SAUCE	○ OTHER	○ SIDE SALAD	○ OTHER

NOTES

WOULD YOU GO BACK?		OVERALL RATING
○ YES	○ NO	/ 10

BURGER LOGBOOK

DATE	
BURGER JOINT	
LOCATION	COST $
BURGER STYLE	

TOPPINGS		TYPE OF BEEF	
○ LETTUCE	○ ONION		
○ BACON	○ PICKLES	**TYPE OF BUN**	
○ TOMATO	○ CHEESE		
○ EGG	○ CHILI	**COOKED**	
○ AVOCADO	○ MUSHROOMS	○ PAN-FRIED	○ SMASHED BURGER
○ CHILES	○ OTHER	○ STEAMED	○ BROILED
CONDIMENTS		○ CHAR-GRILLED	○ OTHER
○ KETCHUP	○ MUSTARD	**SIDES**	
○ THOUSAND ISLAND	○ MAYONNAISE	○ FRENCH FRIES	○ ZUCCHINI FRIES
○ RANCH	○ RELISH	○ ONION RINGS	○ SWEET POTATO FRIES
○ BBQ SAUCE	○ OTHER	○ SIDE SALAD	○ OTHER

NOTES

WOULD YOU GO BACK?		OVERALL RATING
○ YES	○ NO	/ 10

BURGER LOGBOOK

DATE	
BURGER JOINT	
LOCATION	COST $
BURGER STYLE	

TOPPINGS	
○ LETTUCE	○ ONION
○ BACON	○ PICKLES
○ TOMATO	○ CHEESE
○ EGG	○ CHILI
○ AVOCADO	○ MUSHROOMS
○ CHILES	○ OTHER

CONDIMENTS	
○ KETCHUP	○ MUSTARD
○ THOUSAND ISLAND	○ MAYONNAISE
○ RANCH	○ RELISH
○ BBQ SAUCE	○ OTHER

TYPE OF BEEF

TYPE OF BUN

COOKED	
○ PAN-FRIED	○ SMASHED BURGER
○ STEAMED	○ BROILED
○ CHAR-GRILLED	○ OTHER

SIDES	
○ FRENCH FRIES	○ ZUCCHINI FRIES
○ ONION RINGS	○ SWEET POTATO FRIES
○ SIDE SALAD	○ OTHER

NOTES

WOULD YOU GO BACK?		OVERALL RATING
○ YES	○ NO	/ 10

BURGER LOGBOOK

DATE			
BURGER JOINT			
LOCATION		COST	$
BURGER STYLE			

TOPPINGS

○ LETTUCE	○ ONION
○ BACON	○ PICKLES
○ TOMATO	○ CHEESE
○ EGG	○ CHILI
○ AVOCADO	○ MUSHROOMS
○ CHILES	○ OTHER

CONDIMENTS

○ KETCHUP	○ MUSTARD
○ THOUSAND ISLAND	○ MAYONNAISE
○ RANCH	○ RELISH
○ BBQ SAUCE	○ OTHER

TYPE OF BEEF

TYPE OF BUN

COOKED

○ PAN-FRIED	○ SMASHED BURGER
○ STEAMED	○ BROILED
○ CHAR-GRILLED	○ OTHER

SIDES

○ FRENCH FRIES	○ ZUCCHINI FRIES
○ ONION RINGS	○ SWEET POTATO FRIES
○ SIDE SALAD	○ OTHER

NOTES

WOULD YOU GO BACK?		OVERALL RATING
○ YES	○ NO	/ 10

BURGER LOGBOOK

DATE	
BURGER JOINT	
LOCATION	**COST** $
BURGER STYLE	

TOPPINGS		TYPE OF BEEF	
○ LETTUCE	○ ONION		
○ BACON	○ PICKLES	**TYPE OF BUN**	
○ TOMATO	○ CHEESE		
○ EGG	○ CHILI	**COOKED**	
○ AVOCADO	○ MUSHROOMS	○ PAN-FRIED	○ SMASHED BURGER
○ CHILES	○ OTHER	○ STEAMED	○ BROILED
CONDIMENTS		○ CHAR-GRILLED	○ OTHER
○ KETCHUP	○ MUSTARD	**SIDES**	
○ THOUSAND ISLAND	○ MAYONNAISE	○ FRENCH FRIES	○ ZUCCHINI FRIES
○ RANCH	○ RELISH	○ ONION RINGS	○ SWEET POTATO FRIES
○ BBQ SAUCE	○ OTHER	○ SIDE SALAD	○ OTHER

NOTES

WOULD YOU GO BACK?		OVERALL RATING
○ YES	○ NO	/ 10

BURGER LOGBOOK

DATE			
BURGER JOINT			
LOCATION		COST	$
BURGER STYLE			

TOPPINGS		TYPE OF BEEF	
○ LETTUCE	○ ONION		
○ BACON	○ PICKLES	**TYPE OF BUN**	
○ TOMATO	○ CHEESE		
○ EGG	○ CHILI	**COOKED**	
○ AVOCADO	○ MUSHROOMS	○ PAN-FRIED	○ SMASHED BURGER
○ CHILES	○ OTHER	○ STEAMED	○ BROILED
CONDIMENTS		○ CHAR-GRILLED	○ OTHER
○ KETCHUP	○ MUSTARD	**SIDES**	
○ THOUSAND ISLAND	○ MAYONNAISE	○ FRENCH FRIES	○ ZUCCHINI FRIES
○ RANCH	○ RELISH	○ ONION RINGS	○ SWEET POTATO FRIES
○ BBQ SAUCE	○ OTHER	○ SIDE SALAD	○ OTHER

NOTES

WOULD YOU GO BACK?		OVERALL RATING
○ YES	○ NO	/ 10

BURGER LOGBOOK

DATE	
BURGER JOINT	
LOCATION	COST $
BURGER STYLE	

TOPPINGS		TYPE OF BEEF	
○ LETTUCE	○ ONION		
○ BACON	○ PICKLES	**TYPE OF BUN**	
○ TOMATO	○ CHEESE		
○ EGG	○ CHILI	**COOKED**	
○ AVOCADO	○ MUSHROOMS	○ PAN-FRIED	○ SMASHED BURGER
○ CHILES	○ OTHER	○ STEAMED	○ BROILED

CONDIMENTS		○ CHAR-GRILLED	○ OTHER
○ KETCHUP	○ MUSTARD	**SIDES**	
○ THOUSAND ISLAND	○ MAYONNAISE	○ FRENCH FRIES	○ ZUCCHINI FRIES
○ RANCH	○ RELISH	○ ONION RINGS	○ SWEET POTATO FRIES
○ BBQ SAUCE	○ OTHER	○ SIDE SALAD	○ OTHER

NOTES

WOULD YOU GO BACK?		OVERALL RATING
○ YES	○ NO	/ 10

BURGER LOGBOOK

DATE	
BURGER JOINT	
LOCATION	**COST** $
BURGER STYLE	

TOPPINGS		TYPE OF BEEF

○ LETTUCE	○ ONION	
○ BACON	○ PICKLES	**TYPE OF BUN**
○ TOMATO	○ CHEESE	
○ EGG	○ CHILI	**COOKED**
○ AVOCADO	○ MUSHROOMS	○ PAN-FRIED / ○ SMASHED BURGER
○ CHILES	○ OTHER	○ STEAMED / ○ BROILED

TYPE OF BEEF

TYPE OF BUN

COOKED

○ PAN-FRIED	○ SMASHED BURGER
○ STEAMED	○ BROILED
○ CHAR-GRILLED	○ OTHER

CONDIMENTS

○ KETCHUP	○ MUSTARD
○ THOUSAND ISLAND	○ MAYONNAISE
○ RANCH	○ RELISH
○ BBQ SAUCE	○ OTHER

SIDES

○ FRENCH FRIES	○ ZUCCHINI FRIES
○ ONION RINGS	○ SWEET POTATO FRIES
○ SIDE SALAD	○ OTHER

NOTES

WOULD YOU GO BACK?		OVERALL RATING
○ YES	○ NO	/ 10

BURGER LOGBOOK

DATE	
BURGER JOINT	

LOCATION		COST	$

BURGER STYLE	

TOPPINGS		TYPE OF BEEF	
○ LETTUCE	○ ONION		

		TYPE OF BUN	
○ BACON	○ PICKLES		
○ TOMATO	○ CHEESE		

		COOKED	
○ EGG	○ CHILI		
○ AVOCADO	○ MUSHROOMS	○ PAN-FRIED	○ SMASHED BURGER
○ CHILES	○ OTHER	○ STEAMED	○ BROILED

CONDIMENTS		○ CHAR-GRILLED	○ OTHER
○ KETCHUP	○ MUSTARD	**SIDES**	
○ THOUSAND ISLAND	○ MAYONNAISE	○ FRENCH FRIES	○ ZUCCHINI FRIES
○ RANCH	○ RELISH	○ ONION RINGS	○ SWEET POTATO FRIES
○ BBQ SAUCE	○ OTHER	○ SIDE SALAD	○ OTHER

NOTES

WOULD YOU GO BACK?		OVERALL RATING
○ YES	○ NO	/ 10

BURGER LOGBOOK

DATE			
BURGER JOINT			
LOCATION		COST	$
BURGER STYLE			

TOPPINGS

○ LETTUCE	○ ONION
○ BACON	○ PICKLES
○ TOMATO	○ CHEESE
○ EGG	○ CHILI
○ AVOCADO	○ MUSHROOMS
○ CHILES	○ OTHER

CONDIMENTS

○ KETCHUP	○ MUSTARD
○ THOUSAND ISLAND	○ MAYONNAISE
○ RANCH	○ RELISH
○ BBQ SAUCE	○ OTHER

TYPE OF BEEF

TYPE OF BUN

COOKED

○ PAN-FRIED	○ SMASHED BURGER
○ STEAMED	○ BROILED
○ CHAR-GRILLED	○ OTHER

SIDES

○ FRENCH FRIES	○ ZUCCHINI FRIES
○ ONION RINGS	○ SWEET POTATO FRIES
○ SIDE SALAD	○ OTHER

NOTES

WOULD YOU GO BACK?		OVERALL RATING
○ YES	○ NO	/ 10

BURGER LOGBOOK

DATE	
BURGER JOINT	
LOCATION	COST $
BURGER STYLE	

TOPPINGS

○ LETTUCE	○ ONION
○ BACON	○ PICKLES
○ TOMATO	○ CHEESE
○ EGG	○ CHILI
○ AVOCADO	○ MUSHROOMS
○ CHILES	○ OTHER

CONDIMENTS

○ KETCHUP	○ MUSTARD
○ THOUSAND ISLAND	○ MAYONNAISE
○ RANCH	○ RELISH
○ BBQ SAUCE	○ OTHER

TYPE OF BEEF

TYPE OF BUN

COOKED

○ PAN-FRIED	○ SMASHED BURGER
○ STEAMED	○ BROILED
○ CHAR-GRILLED	○ OTHER

SIDES

○ FRENCH FRIES	○ ZUCCHINI FRIES
○ ONION RINGS	○ SWEET POTATO FRIES
○ SIDE SALAD	○ OTHER

NOTES

WOULD YOU GO BACK?		OVERALL RATING
○ YES	○ NO	/ 10

BURGER LOGBOOK

DATE	
BURGER JOINT	
LOCATION	COST $
BURGER STYLE	

TOPPINGS

○ LETTUCE	○ ONION
○ BACON	○ PICKLES
○ TOMATO	○ CHEESE
○ EGG	○ CHILI
○ AVOCADO	○ MUSHROOMS
○ CHILES	○ OTHER

CONDIMENTS

○ KETCHUP	○ MUSTARD
○ THOUSAND ISLAND	○ MAYONNAISE
○ RANCH	○ RELISH
○ BBQ SAUCE	○ OTHER

TYPE OF BEEF

TYPE OF BUN

COOKED

○ PAN-FRIED	○ SMASHED BURGER
○ STEAMED	○ BROILED
○ CHAR-GRILLED	○ OTHER

SIDES

○ FRENCH FRIES	○ ZUCCHINI FRIES
○ ONION RINGS	○ SWEET POTATO FRIES
○ SIDE SALAD	○ OTHER

NOTES

WOULD YOU GO BACK?		OVERALL RATING
○ YES	○ NO	/ 10

BURGER LOGBOOK

DATE	
BURGER JOINT	
LOCATION	COST $
BURGER STYLE	

TOPPINGS

○ LETTUCE	○ ONION
○ BACON	○ PICKLES
○ TOMATO	○ CHEESE
○ EGG	○ CHILI
○ AVOCADO	○ MUSHROOMS
○ CHILES	○ OTHER

CONDIMENTS

○ KETCHUP	○ MUSTARD
○ THOUSAND ISLAND	○ MAYONNAISE
○ RANCH	○ RELISH
○ BBQ SAUCE	○ OTHER

TYPE OF BEEF

TYPE OF BUN

COOKED

○ PAN-FRIED	○ SMASHED BURGER
○ STEAMED	○ BROILED
○ CHAR-GRILLED	○ OTHER

SIDES

○ FRENCH FRIES	○ ZUCCHINI FRIES
○ ONION RINGS	○ SWEET POTATO FRIES
○ SIDE SALAD	○ OTHER

NOTES

WOULD YOU GO BACK?		OVERALL RATING
○ YES	○ NO	/ 10

BURGER LOGBOOK

DATE	
BURGER JOINT	
LOCATION	COST $
BURGER STYLE	

TOPPINGS

○ LETTUCE	○ ONION
○ BACON	○ PICKLES
○ TOMATO	○ CHEESE
○ EGG	○ CHILI
○ AVOCADO	○ MUSHROOMS
○ CHILES	○ OTHER

CONDIMENTS

○ KETCHUP	○ MUSTARD
○ THOUSAND ISLAND	○ MAYONNAISE
○ RANCH	○ RELISH
○ BBQ SAUCE	○ OTHER

TYPE OF BEEF

TYPE OF BUN

COOKED

○ PAN-FRIED	○ SMASHED BURGER
○ STEAMED	○ BROILED
○ CHAR-GRILLED	○ OTHER

SIDES

○ FRENCH FRIES	○ ZUCCHINI FRIES
○ ONION RINGS	○ SWEET POTATO FRIES
○ SIDE SALAD	○ OTHER

NOTES

WOULD YOU GO BACK?		OVERALL RATING
○ YES	○ NO	/ 10

BURGER LOGBOOK

DATE	
BURGER JOINT	
LOCATION	COST $
BURGER STYLE	

TOPPINGS	
○ LETTUCE	○ ONION
○ BACON	○ PICKLES
○ TOMATO	○ CHEESE
○ EGG	○ CHILI
○ AVOCADO	○ MUSHROOMS
○ CHILES	○ OTHER

CONDIMENTS	
○ KETCHUP	○ MUSTARD
○ THOUSAND ISLAND	○ MAYONNAISE
○ RANCH	○ RELISH
○ BBQ SAUCE	○ OTHER

TYPE OF BEEF

TYPE OF BUN

COOKED	
○ PAN-FRIED	○ SMASHED BURGER
○ STEAMED	○ BROILED
○ CHAR-GRILLED	○ OTHER

SIDES	
○ FRENCH FRIES	○ ZUCCHINI FRIES
○ ONION RINGS	○ SWEET POTATO FRIES
○ SIDE SALAD	○ OTHER

NOTES

WOULD YOU GO BACK?		OVERALL RATING
○ YES	○ NO	/ 10

BURGER LOGBOOK

DATE			
BURGER JOINT			
LOCATION		COST	$
BURGER STYLE			

TOPPINGS

○ LETTUCE	○ ONION
○ BACON	○ PICKLES
○ TOMATO	○ CHEESE
○ EGG	○ CHILI
○ AVOCADO	○ MUSHROOMS
○ CHILES	○ OTHER

CONDIMENTS

○ KETCHUP	○ MUSTARD
○ THOUSAND ISLAND	○ MAYONNAISE
○ RANCH	○ RELISH
○ BBQ SAUCE	○ OTHER

TYPE OF BEEF

TYPE OF BUN

COOKED

○ PAN-FRIED	○ SMASHED BURGER
○ STEAMED	○ BROILED
○ CHAR-GRILLED	○ OTHER

SIDES

○ FRENCH FRIES	○ ZUCCHINI FRIES
○ ONION RINGS	○ SWEET POTATO FRIES
○ SIDE SALAD	○ OTHER

NOTES

WOULD YOU GO BACK?		OVERALL RATING
○ YES	○ NO	/ 10

BURGER LOGBOOK

DATE	
BURGER JOINT	

LOCATION		COST	$

BURGER STYLE	

TOPPINGS	
○ LETTUCE	○ ONION
○ BACON	○ PICKLES
○ TOMATO	○ CHEESE
○ EGG	○ CHILI
○ AVOCADO	○ MUSHROOMS
○ CHILES	○ OTHER

CONDIMENTS	
○ KETCHUP	○ MUSTARD
○ THOUSAND ISLAND	○ MAYONNAISE
○ RANCH	○ RELISH
○ BBQ SAUCE	○ OTHER

TYPE OF BEEF

TYPE OF BUN

COOKED	
○ PAN-FRIED	○ SMASHED BURGER
○ STEAMED	○ BROILED
○ CHAR-GRILLED	○ OTHER

SIDES	
○ FRENCH FRIES	○ ZUCCHINI FRIES
○ ONION RINGS	○ SWEET POTATO FRIES
○ SIDE SALAD	○ OTHER

NOTES

WOULD YOU GO BACK?		OVERALL RATING
○ YES	○ NO	/ 10

BURGER LOGBOOK

DATE	
BURGER JOINT	
LOCATION	COST $
BURGER STYLE	

TOPPINGS		TYPE OF BEEF	
○ LETTUCE	○ ONION		
○ BACON	○ PICKLES	**TYPE OF BUN**	
○ TOMATO	○ CHEESE		
○ EGG	○ CHILI	**COOKED**	
○ AVOCADO	○ MUSHROOMS	○ PAN-FRIED	○ SMASHED BURGER
○ CHILES	○ OTHER	○ STEAMED	○ BROILED

CONDIMENTS		○ CHAR-GRILLED	○ OTHER
○ KETCHUP	○ MUSTARD	**SIDES**	
○ THOUSAND ISLAND	○ MAYONNAISE	○ FRENCH FRIES	○ ZUCCHINI FRIES
○ RANCH	○ RELISH	○ ONION RINGS	○ SWEET POTATO FRIES
○ BBQ SAUCE	○ OTHER	○ SIDE SALAD	○ OTHER

NOTES

WOULD YOU GO BACK?		OVERALL RATING
○ YES	○ NO	/ 10

BURGER LOGBOOK

DATE	
BURGER JOINT	
LOCATION	COST $
BURGER STYLE	

TOPPINGS

○ LETTUCE	○ ONION
○ BACON	○ PICKLES
○ TOMATO	○ CHEESE
○ EGG	○ CHILI
○ AVOCADO	○ MUSHROOMS
○ CHILES	○ OTHER

CONDIMENTS

○ KETCHUP	○ MUSTARD
○ THOUSAND ISLAND	○ MAYONNAISE
○ RANCH	○ RELISH
○ BBQ SAUCE	○ OTHER

TYPE OF BEEF

TYPE OF BUN

COOKED

○ PAN-FRIED	○ SMASHED BURGER
○ STEAMED	○ BROILED
○ CHAR-GRILLED	○ OTHER

SIDES

○ FRENCH FRIES	○ ZUCCHINI FRIES
○ ONION RINGS	○ SWEET POTATO FRIES
○ SIDE SALAD	○ OTHER

NOTES

WOULD YOU GO BACK?		OVERALL RATING
○ YES	○ NO	/ 10

BURGER LOGBOOK

DATE			
BURGER JOINT			
LOCATION		COST	$
BURGER STYLE			

TOPPINGS

○ LETTUCE	○ ONION
○ BACON	○ PICKLES
○ TOMATO	○ CHEESE
○ EGG	○ CHILI
○ AVOCADO	○ MUSHROOMS
○ CHILES	○ OTHER

CONDIMENTS

○ KETCHUP	○ MUSTARD
○ THOUSAND ISLAND	○ MAYONNAISE
○ RANCH	○ RELISH
○ BBQ SAUCE	○ OTHER

TYPE OF BEEF

TYPE OF BUN

COOKED

○ PAN-FRIED	○ SMASHED BURGER
○ STEAMED	○ BROILED
○ CHAR-GRILLED	○ OTHER

SIDES

○ FRENCH FRIES	○ ZUCCHINI FRIES
○ ONION RINGS	○ SWEET POTATO FRIES
○ SIDE SALAD	○ OTHER

NOTES

WOULD YOU GO BACK?		OVERALL RATING
○ YES	○ NO	/ 10

BURGER LOGBOOK

DATE	
BURGER JOINT	
LOCATION	COST $
BURGER STYLE	

TOPPINGS	
○ LETTUCE	○ ONION
○ BACON	○ PICKLES
○ TOMATO	○ CHEESE
○ EGG	○ CHILI
○ AVOCADO	○ MUSHROOMS
○ CHILES	○ OTHER

CONDIMENTS	
○ KETCHUP	○ MUSTARD
○ THOUSAND ISLAND	○ MAYONNAISE
○ RANCH	○ RELISH
○ BBQ SAUCE	○ OTHER

TYPE OF BEEF

TYPE OF BUN

COOKED	
○ PAN-FRIED	○ SMASHED BURGER
○ STEAMED	○ BROILED
○ CHAR-GRILLED	○ OTHER

SIDES	
○ FRENCH FRIES	○ ZUCCHINI FRIES
○ ONION RINGS	○ SWEET POTATO FRIES
○ SIDE SALAD	○ OTHER

NOTES

WOULD YOU GO BACK?		OVERALL RATING
○ YES	○ NO	/ 10

BURGER LOGBOOK

DATE	
BURGER JOINT	

LOCATION		COST	$

BURGER STYLE	

TOPPINGS	
○ LETTUCE	○ ONION
○ BACON	○ PICKLES
○ TOMATO	○ CHEESE
○ EGG	○ CHILI
○ AVOCADO	○ MUSHROOMS
○ CHILES	○ OTHER

CONDIMENTS	
○ KETCHUP	○ MUSTARD
○ THOUSAND ISLAND	○ MAYONNAISE
○ RANCH	○ RELISH
○ BBQ SAUCE	○ OTHER

TYPE OF BEEF

TYPE OF BUN

COOKED	
○ PAN-FRIED	○ SMASHED BURGER
○ STEAMED	○ BROILED
○ CHAR-GRILLED	○ OTHER

SIDES	
○ FRENCH FRIES	○ ZUCCHINI FRIES
○ ONION RINGS	○ SWEET POTATO FRIES
○ SIDE SALAD	○ OTHER

NOTES

WOULD YOU GO BACK?		OVERALL RATING
○ YES	○ NO	/ 10

BURGER LOGBOOK

DATE	
BURGER JOINT	
LOCATION	COST $
BURGER STYLE	

TOPPINGS

○ LETTUCE	○ ONION
○ BACON	○ PICKLES
○ TOMATO	○ CHEESE
○ EGG	○ CHILI
○ AVOCADO	○ MUSHROOMS
○ CHILES	○ OTHER

CONDIMENTS

○ KETCHUP	○ MUSTARD
○ THOUSAND ISLAND	○ MAYONNAISE
○ RANCH	○ RELISH
○ BBQ SAUCE	○ OTHER

TYPE OF BEEF

TYPE OF BUN

COOKED

○ PAN-FRIED	○ SMASHED BURGER
○ STEAMED	○ BROILED
○ CHAR-GRILLED	○ OTHER

SIDES

○ FRENCH FRIES	○ ZUCCHINI FRIES
○ ONION RINGS	○ SWEET POTATO FRIES
○ SIDE SALAD	○ OTHER

NOTES

WOULD YOU GO BACK?	**OVERALL RATING**
○ YES ○ NO	/ 10

BURGER LOGBOOK

DATE	
BURGER JOINT	
LOCATION	COST $
BURGER STYLE	

TOPPINGS

○ LETTUCE	○ ONION
○ BACON	○ PICKLES
○ TOMATO	○ CHEESE
○ EGG	○ CHILI
○ AVOCADO	○ MUSHROOMS
○ CHILES	○ OTHER

CONDIMENTS

○ KETCHUP	○ MUSTARD
○ THOUSAND ISLAND	○ MAYONNAISE
○ RANCH	○ RELISH
○ BBQ SAUCE	○ OTHER

TYPE OF BEEF

TYPE OF BUN

COOKED

○ PAN-FRIED	○ SMASHED BURGER
○ STEAMED	○ BROILED
○ CHAR-GRILLED	○ OTHER

SIDES

○ FRENCH FRIES	○ ZUCCHINI FRIES
○ ONION RINGS	○ SWEET POTATO FRIES
○ SIDE SALAD	○ OTHER

NOTES

WOULD YOU GO BACK?		OVERALL RATING
○ YES	○ NO	/ 10

BURGER LOGBOOK

DATE	
BURGER JOINT	

LOCATION		COST	$

BURGER STYLE	

TOPPINGS

○ LETTUCE	○ ONION
○ BACON	○ PICKLES
○ TOMATO	○ CHEESE
○ EGG	○ CHILI
○ AVOCADO	○ MUSHROOMS
○ CHILES	○ OTHER

CONDIMENTS

○ KETCHUP	○ MUSTARD
○ THOUSAND ISLAND	○ MAYONNAISE
○ RANCH	○ RELISH
○ BBQ SAUCE	○ OTHER

TYPE OF BEEF

TYPE OF BUN

COOKED

○ PAN-FRIED	○ SMASHED BURGER
○ STEAMED	○ BROILED
○ CHAR-GRILLED	○ OTHER

SIDES

○ FRENCH FRIES	○ ZUCCHINI FRIES
○ ONION RINGS	○ SWEET POTATO FRIES
○ SIDE SALAD	○ OTHER

NOTES

WOULD YOU GO BACK?		OVERALL RATING
○ YES	○ NO	/ 10

BURGER LOGBOOK

DATE	
BURGER JOINT	
LOCATION	COST $
BURGER STYLE	

TOPPINGS

○ LETTUCE	○ CNION
○ BACON	○ PICKLES
○ TOMATO	○ CHEESE
○ EGG	○ CHILI
○ AVOCADO	○ MUSHROOMS
○ CHILES	○ OTHER

CONDIMENTS

○ KETCHUP	○ MUSTARD
○ THOUSAND ISLAND	○ MAYONNAISE
○ RANCH	○ RELISH
○ BBQ SAUCE	○ OTHER

TYPE OF BEEF

TYPE OF BUN

COOKED

○ PAN-FRIED	○ SMASHED BURGER
○ STEAMED	○ BROILED
○ CHAR-GRILLED	○ OTHER

SIDES

○ FRENCH FRIES	○ ZUCCHINI FRIES
○ ONION RINGS	○ SWEET POTATO FRIES
○ SIDE SALAD	○ OTHER

NOTES

WOULD YOU GO BACK?		OVERALL RATING
○ YES	○ NO	/ 10

BURGER LOGBOOK

DATE	
BURGER JOINT	
LOCATION	COST $
BURGER STYLE	

TOPPINGS	
○ LETTUCE	○ ONION
○ BACON	○ PICKLES
○ TOMATO	○ CHEESE
○ EGG	○ CHILI
○ AVOCADO	○ MUSHROOMS
○ CHILES	○ OTHER

CONDIMENTS	
○ KETCHUP	○ MUSTARD
○ THOUSAND ISLAND	○ MAYONNAISE
○ RANCH	○ RELISH
○ BBQ SAUCE	○ OTHER

TYPE OF BEEF

TYPE OF BUN

COOKED	
○ PAN-FRIED	○ SMASHED BURGER
○ STEAMED	○ BROILED
○ CHAR-GRILLED	○ OTHER

SIDES	
○ FRENCH FRIES	○ ZUCCHINI FRIES
○ ONION RINGS	○ SWEET POTATO FRIES
○ SIDE SALAD	○ OTHER

NOTES

WOULD YOU GO BACK?		OVERALL RATING
○ YES	○ NO	/ 10

BURGER LOGBOOK

DATE	
BURGER JOINT	

LOCATION		COST	$

BURGER STYLE	

TOPPINGS	
○ LETTUCE	○ ONION
○ BACON	○ PICKLES
○ TOMATO	○ CHEESE
○ EGG	○ CHILI
○ AVOCADO	○ MUSHROOMS
○ CHILES	○ OTHER

CONDIMENTS	
○ KETCHUP	○ MUSTARD
○ THOUSAND ISLAND	○ MAYONNAISE
○ RANCH	○ RELISH
○ BBQ SAUCE	○ OTHER

TYPE OF BEEF

TYPE OF BUN

COOKED	
○ PAN-FRIED	○ SMASHED BURGER
○ STEAMED	○ BROILED
○ CHAR-GRILLED	○ OTHER

SIDES	
○ FRENCH FRIES	○ ZUCCHINI FRIES
○ ONION RINGS	○ SWEET POTATO FRIES
○ SIDE SALAD	○ OTHER

NOTES

WOULD YOU GO BACK?		OVERALL RATING
○ YES	○ NO	/ 10

BURGER LOGBOOK

DATE	
BURGER JOINT	
LOCATION	COST \$
BURGER STYLE	

TOPPINGS

○ LETTUCE	○ ONION
○ BACON	○ PICKLES
○ TOMATO	○ CHEESE
○ EGG	○ CHILI
○ AVOCADO	○ MUSHROOMS
○ CHILES	○ OTHER

CONDIMENTS

○ KETCHUP	○ MUSTARD
○ THOUSAND ISLAND	○ MAYONNAISE
○ RANCH	○ RELISH
○ BBQ SAUCE	○ OTHER

TYPE OF BEEF

TYPE OF BUN

COOKED

○ PAN-FRIED	○ SMASHED BURGER
○ STEAMED	○ BROILED
○ CHAR-GRILLED	○ OTHER

SIDES

○ FRENCH FRIES	○ ZUCCHINI FRIES
○ ONION RINGS	○ SWEET POTATO FRIES
○ SIDE SALAD	○ OTHER

NOTES

WOULD YOU GO BACK?		OVERALL RATING
○ YES	○ NO	/ 10

BURGER LOGBOOK

DATE	
BURGER JOINT	
LOCATION	COST $
BURGER STYLE	

TOPPINGS		TYPE OF BEEF	
○ LETTUCE	○ ONION		

TYPE OF BUN

TOPPINGS	
○ BACON	○ PICKLES
○ TOMATO	○ CHEESE
○ EGG	○ CHILI
○ AVOCADO	○ MUSHROOMS
○ CHILES	○ OTHER

COOKED	
○ PAN-FRIED	○ SMASHED BURGER
○ STEAMED	○ BROILED
○ CHAR-GRILLED	○ OTHER

CONDIMENTS	
○ KETCHUP	○ MUSTARD
○ THOUSAND ISLAND	○ MAYONNAISE
○ RANCH	○ RELISH
○ BBQ SAUCE	○ OTHER

SIDES	
○ FRENCH FRIES	○ ZUCCHINI FRIES
○ ONION RINGS	○ SWEET POTATO FRIES
○ SIDE SALAD	○ OTHER

NOTES

WOULD YOU GO BACK?		OVERALL RATING
○ YES	○ NO	/ 10

BURGER LOGBOOK

DATE	
BURGER JOINT	
LOCATION	**COST** $
BURGER STYLE	

TOPPINGS		TYPE OF BEEF	
○ LETTUCE	○ ONION		
○ BACON	○ PICKLES	TYPE OF BUN	
○ TOMATO	○ CHEESE		
○ EGG	○ CHILI	COOKED	
○ AVOCADO	○ MUSHROOMS	○ PAN-FRIED	○ SMASHED BURGER
○ CHILES	○ OTHER	○ STEAMED	○ BROILED
CONDIMENTS		○ CHAR-GRILLED	○ OTHER
○ KETCHUP	○ MUSTARD	SIDES	
○ THOUSAND ISLAND	○ MAYONNAISE	○ FRENCH FRIES	○ ZUCCHINI FRIES
○ RANCH	○ RELISH	○ ONION RINGS	○ SWEET POTATO FRIES
○ BBQ SAUCE	○ OTHER	○ SIDE SALAD	○ OTHER

NOTES

WOULD YOU GO BACK?		OVERALL RATING
○ YES	○ NO	/ 10

BURGER LOGBOOK

DATE	
BURGER JOINT	
LOCATION	COST $
BURGER STYLE	

TOPPINGS		TYPE OF BEEF	
○ LETTUCE	○ CNION		
○ BACON	○ PICKLES	**TYPE OF BUN**	
○ TOMATO	○ CHEESE		
○ EGG	○ CHILI	**COOKED**	
○ AVOCADO	○ MUSHROOMS	○ PAN-FRIED	○ SMASHED BURGER
○ CHILES	○ OTHER	○ STEAMED	○ BROILED
CONDIMENTS		○ CHAR-GRILLED	○ OTHER
○ KETCHUP	○ MUSTARD	**SIDES**	
○ THOUSAND ISLAND	○ MAYONNAISE	○ FRENCH FRIES	○ ZUCCHINI FRIES
○ RANCH	○ RELISH	○ ONION RINGS	○ SWEET POTATO FRIES
○ BBQ SAUCE	○ OTHER	○ SIDE SALAD	○ OTHER

NOTES

WOULD YOU GO BACK?		OVERALL RATING
○ YES	○ NO	/ 10

BURGER LOGBOOK

DATE	
BURGER JOINT	
LOCATION	COST $
BURGER STYLE	

TOPPINGS

○ LETTUCE	○ ONION
○ BACON	○ PICKLES
○ TOMATO	○ CHEESE
○ EGG	○ CHILI
○ AVOCADO	○ MUSHROOMS
○ CHILES	○ OTHER

CONDIMENTS

○ KETCHUP	○ MUSTARD
○ THOUSAND ISLAND	○ MAYONNAISE
○ RANCH	○ RELISH
○ BBQ SAUCE	○ OTHER

TYPE OF BEEF

TYPE OF BUN

COOKED

○ PAN-FRIED	○ SMASHED BURGER
○ STEAMED	○ BROILED
○ CHAR-GRILLED	○ OTHER

SIDES

○ FRENCH FRIES	○ ZUCCHINI FRIES
○ ONION RINGS	○ SWEET POTATO FRIES
○ SIDE SALAD	○ OTHER

NOTES

WOULD YOU GO BACK?		OVERALL RATING
○ YES	○ NO	/ 10

BURGER LOGBOOK

DATE	
BURGER JOINT	
LOCATION	COST $
BURGER STYLE	

TOPPINGS	
○ LETTUCE	○ ONION
○ BACON	○ PICKLES
○ TOMATO	○ CHEESE
○ EGG	○ CHILI
○ AVOCADO	○ MUSHROOMS
○ CHILES	○ OTHER

CONDIMENTS	
○ KETCHUP	○ MUSTARD
○ THOUSAND ISLAND	○ MAYONNAISE
○ RANCH	○ RELISH
○ BBQ SAUCE	○ OTHER

TYPE OF BEEF

TYPE OF BUN

COOKED	
○ PAN-FRIED	○ SMASHED BURGER
○ STEAMED	○ BROILED
○ CHAR-GRILLED	○ OTHER

SIDES	
○ FRENCH FRIES	○ ZUCCHINI FRIES
○ ONION RINGS	○ SWEET POTATO FRIES
○ SIDE SALAD	○ OTHER

NOTES

WOULD YOU GO BACK?		OVERALL RATING
○ YES	○ NO	/ 10

BURGER LOGBOOK

DATE	
BURGER JOINT	
LOCATION	COST $
BURGER STYLE	

TOPPINGS	
○ LETTUCE	○ ONION
○ BACON	○ PICKLES
○ TOMATO	○ CHEESE
○ EGG	○ CHILI
○ AVOCADO	○ MUSHROOMS
○ CHILES	○ OTHER

CONDIMENTS	
○ KETCHUP	○ MUSTARD
○ THOUSAND ISLAND	○ MAYONNAISE
○ RANCH	○ RELISH
○ BBQ SAUCE	○ OTHER

TYPE OF BEEF

TYPE OF BUN

COOKED	
○ PAN-FRIED	○ SMASHED BURGER
○ STEAMED	○ BROILED
○ CHAR-GRILLED	○ OTHER

SIDES	
○ FRENCH FRIES	○ ZUCCHINI FRIES
○ ONION RINGS	○ SWEET POTATO FRIES
○ SIDE SALAD	○ OTHER

NOTES

WOULD YOU GO BACK?		OVERALL RATING
○ YES	○ NO	/ 10

BURGER LOGBOOK

DATE	
BURGER JOINT	
LOCATION	COST $
BURGER STYLE	

TOPPINGS	
○ LETTUCE	○ ONION
○ BACON	○ PICKLES
○ TOMATO	○ CHEESE
○ EGG	○ CHILI
○ AVOCADO	○ MUSHROOMS
○ CHILES	○ OTHER

CONDIMENTS	
○ KETCHUP	○ MUSTARD
○ THOUSAND ISLAND	○ MAYONNAISE
○ RANCH	○ RELISH
○ BBQ SAUCE	○ OTHER

TYPE OF BEEF

TYPE OF BUN

COOKED	
○ PAN-FRIED	○ SMASHED BURGER
○ STEAMED	○ BROILED
○ CHAR-GRILLED	○ OTHER

SIDES	
○ FRENCH FRIES	○ ZUCCHINI FRIES
○ ONION RINGS	○ SWEET POTATO FRIES
○ SIDE SALAD	○ OTHER

NOTES

WOULD YOU GO BACK?		OVERALL RATING
○ YES	○ NO	/ 10

BURGER LOGBOOK

DATE	
BURGER JOINT	
LOCATION	COST $
BURGER STYLE	

TOPPINGS

○ LETTUCE	○ ONION
○ BACON	○ PICKLES
○ TOMATO	○ CHEESE
○ EGG	○ CHILI
○ AVOCADO	○ MUSHROOMS
○ CHILES	○ OTHER

CONDIMENTS

○ KETCHUP	○ MUSTARD
○ THOUSAND ISLAND	○ MAYONNAISE
○ RANCH	○ RELISH
○ BBQ SAUCE	○ OTHER

TYPE OF BEEF

TYPE OF BUN

COOKED

○ PAN-FRIED	○ SMASHED BURGER
○ STEAMED	○ BROILED
○ CHAR-GRILLED	○ OTHER

SIDES

○ FRENCH FRIES	○ ZUCCHINI FRIES
○ ONION RINGS	○ SWEET POTATO FRIES
○ SIDE SALAD	○ OTHER

NOTES

WOULD YOU GO BACK?		OVERALL RATING
○ YES	○ NO	/ 10

BURGER LOGBOOK

DATE	
BURGER JOINT	
LOCATION	**COST** $
BURGER STYLE	

TOPPINGS

○ LETTUCE	○ CNION
○ BACON	○ PICKLES
○ TOMATO	○ CHEESE
○ EGG	○ CHILI
○ AVOCADO	○ MUSHROOMS
○ CHILES	○ OTHER

CONDIMENTS

○ KETCHUP	○ MUSTARD
○ THOUSAND ISLAND	○ MAYONNAISE
○ RANCH	○ RELISH
○ BBQ SAUCE	○ OTHER

TYPE OF BEEF

TYPE OF BUN

COOKED

○ PAN-FRIED	○ SMASHED BURGER
○ STEAMED	○ BROILED
○ CHAR-GRILLED	○ OTHER

SIDES

○ FRENCH FRIES	○ ZUCCHINI FRIES
○ ONION RINGS	○ SWEET POTATO FRIES
○ SIDE SALAD	○ OTHER

NOTES

WOULD YOU GO BACK?		OVERALL RATING
○ YES	○ NO	/ 10

BURGER LOGBOOK

DATE	
BURGER JOINT	
LOCATION	COST $
BURGER STYLE	

TOPPINGS		TYPE OF BEEF

○ LETTUCE	○ ONION
○ BACON	○ PICKLES
○ TOMATO	○ CHEESE
○ EGG	○ CHILI
○ AVOCADO	○ MUSHROOMS
○ CHILES	○ OTHER

TYPE OF BUN

COOKED

○ PAN-FRIED	○ SMASHED BURGER
○ STEAMED	○ BROILED
○ CHAR-GRILLED	○ OTHER

CONDIMENTS

○ KETCHUP	○ MUSTARD
○ THOUSAND ISLAND	○ MAYONNAISE
○ RANCH	○ RELISH
○ BBQ SAUCE	○ OTHER

SIDES

○ FRENCH FRIES	○ ZUCCHINI FRIES
○ ONION RINGS	○ SWEET POTATO FRIES
○ SIDE SALAD	○ OTHER

NOTES

WOULD YOU GO BACK?		OVERALL RATING
○ YES	○ NO	/ 10

BURGER LOGBOOK

DATE			
BURGER JOINT			
LOCATION		COST	$
BURGER STYLE			

TOPPINGS

○ LETTUCE	○ ONION
○ BACON	○ PICKLES
○ TOMATO	○ CHEESE
○ EGG	○ CHILI
○ AVOCADO	○ MUSHROOMS
○ CHILES	○ OTHER

CONDIMENTS

○ KETCHUP	○ MUSTARD
○ THOUSAND ISLAND	○ MAYONNAISE
○ RANCH	○ RELISH
○ BBQ SAUCE	○ OTHER

TYPE OF BEEF

TYPE OF BUN

COOKED

○ PAN-FRIED	○ SMASHED BURGER
○ STEAMED	○ BROILED
○ CHAR-GRILLED	○ OTHER

SIDES

○ FRENCH FRIES	○ ZUCCHINI FRIES
○ ONION RINGS	○ SWEET POTATO FRIES
○ SIDE SALAD	○ OTHER

NOTES

WOULD YOU GO BACK?		OVERALL RATING
○ YES	○ NO	/ 10

BURGER LOGBOOK

DATE	
BURGER JOINT	
LOCATION	COST $
BURGER STYLE	

TOPPINGS

○ LETTUCE	○ ONION
○ BACON	○ PICKLES
○ TOMATO	○ CHEESE
○ EGG	○ CHILI
○ AVOCADO	○ MUSHROOMS
○ CHILES	○ OTHER

CONDIMENTS

○ KETCHUP	○ MUSTARD
○ THOUSAND ISLAND	○ MAYONNAISE
○ RANCH	○ RELISH
○ BBQ SAUCE	○ OTHER

TYPE OF BEEF

TYPE OF BUN

COOKED

○ PAN-FRIED	○ SMASHED BURGER
○ STEAMED	○ BROILED
○ CHAR-GRILLED	○ OTHER

SIDES

○ FRENCH FRIES	○ ZUCCHINI FRIES
○ ONION RINGS	○ SWEET POTATO FRIES
○ SIDE SALAD	○ OTHER

NOTES

WOULD YOU GO BACK?

○ YES	○ NO

OVERALL RATING

/ 10

BURGER LOGBOOK

DATE	
BURGER JOINT	
LOCATION	COST $
BURGER STYLE	

TOPPINGS		TYPE OF BEEF	
○ LETTUCE	○ ONION		
○ BACON	○ PICKLES	TYPE OF BUN	
○ TOMATO	○ CHEESE		
○ EGG	○ CHILI	COOKED	
○ AVOCADO	○ MUSHROOMS	○ PAN-FRIED	○ SMASHED BURGER
○ CHILES	○ OTHER	○ STEAMED	○ BROILED

CONDIMENTS		○ CHAR-GRILLED	○ OTHER
○ KETCHUP	○ MUSTARD	SIDES	
○ THOUSAND ISLAND	○ MAYONNAISE	○ FRENCH FRIES	○ ZUCCHINI FRIES
○ RANCH	○ RELISH	○ ONION RINGS	○ SWEET POTATO FRIES
○ BBQ SAUCE	○ OTHER	○ SIDE SALAD	○ OTHER

NOTES

WOULD YOU GO BACK?		OVERALL RATING
○ YES	○ NO	/ 10

BURGER LOGBOOK

DATE	
BURGER JOINT	
LOCATION	COST $
BURGER STYLE	

TOPPINGS

○ LETTUCE	○ ONION
○ BACON	○ PICKLES
○ TOMATO	○ CHEESE
○ EGG	○ CHILI
○ AVOCADO	○ MUSHROOMS
○ CHILES	○ OTHER

CONDIMENTS

○ KETCHUP	○ MUSTARD
○ THOUSAND ISLAND	○ MAYONNAISE
○ RANCH	○ RELISH
○ BBQ SAUCE	○ OTHER

TYPE OF BEEF

TYPE OF BUN

COOKED

○ PAN-FRIED	○ SMASHED BURGER
○ STEAMED	○ BROILED
○ CHAR-GRILLED	○ OTHER

SIDES

○ FRENCH FRIES	○ ZUCCHINI FRIES
○ ONION RINGS	○ SWEET POTATO FRIES
○ SIDE SALAD	○ OTHER

NOTES

WOULD YOU GO BACK?		OVERALL RATING
○ YES	○ NO	/ 10

BURGER LOGBOOK

DATE	
BURGER JOINT	
LOCATION	COST $
BURGER STYLE	

TOPPINGS		TYPE OF BEEF

○ LETTUCE	○ ONION
○ BACON	○ PICKLES
○ TOMATO	○ CHEESE
○ EGG	○ CHILI
○ AVOCADO	○ MUSHROOMS
○ CHILES	○ OTHER

TYPE OF BUN

CONDIMENTS

COOKED

○ KETCHUP	○ MUSTARD
○ THOUSAND ISLAND	○ MAYONNAISE
○ RANCH	○ RELISH
○ BBQ SAUCE	○ OTHER

○ PAN-FRIED	○ SMASHED BURGER
○ STEAMED	○ BROILED
○ CHAR-GRILLED	○ OTHER

SIDES

○ FRENCH FRIES	○ ZUCCHINI FRIES
○ ONION RINGS	○ SWEET POTATO FRIES
○ SIDE SALAD	○ OTHER

NOTES

WOULD YOU GO BACK?		OVERALL RATING
○ YES	○ NO	/ 10

BURGER LOGBOOK

DATE			
BURGER JOINT			
LOCATION		COST	$
BURGER STYLE			

TOPPINGS	
○ LETTUCE	○ ONION
○ BACON	○ PICKLES
○ TOMATO	○ CHEESE
○ EGG	○ CHILI
○ AVOCADO	○ MUSHROOMS
○ CHILES	○ OTHER

CONDIMENTS	
○ KETCHUP	○ MUSTARD
○ THOUSAND ISLAND	○ MAYONNAISE
○ RANCH	○ RELISH
○ BBQ SAUCE	○ OTHER

TYPE OF BEEF

TYPE OF BUN

COOKED	
○ PAN-FRIED	○ SMASHED BURGER
○ STEAMED	○ BROILED
○ CHAR-GRILLED	○ OTHER

SIDES	
○ FRENCH FRIES	○ ZUCCHINI FRIES
○ ONION RINGS	○ SWEET POTATO FRIES
○ SIDE SALAD	○ OTHER

NOTES

WOULD YOU GO BACK?		OVERALL RATING
○ YES	○ NO	/ 10

BURGER LOGBOOK

DATE	
BURGER JOINT	

LOCATION		COST	$

BURGER STYLE	

TOPPINGS	
○ LETTUCE	○ ONION
○ BACON	○ PICKLES
○ TOMATO	○ CHEESE
○ EGG	○ CHILI
○ AVOCADO	○ MUSHROOMS
○ CHILES	○ OTHER

CONDIMENTS	
○ KETCHUP	○ MUSTARD
○ THOUSAND ISLAND	○ MAYONNAISE
○ RANCH	○ RELISH
○ BBQ SAUCE	○ OTHER

TYPE OF BEEF

TYPE OF BUN

COOKED	
○ PAN-FRIED	○ SMASHED BURGER
○ STEAMED	○ BROILED
○ CHAR-GRILLED	○ OTHER

SIDES	
○ FRENCH FRIES	○ ZUCCHINI FRIES
○ ONION RINGS	○ SWEET POTATO FRIES
○ SIDE SALAD	○ OTHER

NOTES

WOULD YOU GO BACK?		OVERALL RATING
○ YES	○ NO	/ 10

BURGER LOGBOOK

DATE	
BURGER JOINT	

LOCATION ,		COST	$

BURGER STYLE	

TOPPINGS	
○ LETTUCE	○ ONION
○ BACON	○ PICKLES
○ TOMATO	○ CHEESE
○ EGG	○ CHILI
○ AVOCADO	○ MUSHROOMS
○ CHILES	○ OTHER

CONDIMENTS	
○ KETCHUP	○ MUSTARD
○ THOUSAND ISLAND	○ MAYONNAISE
○ RANCH	○ RELISH
○ BBQ SAUCE	○ OTHER

TYPE OF BEEF

TYPE OF BUN

COOKED	
○ PAN-FRIED	○ SMASHED BURGER
○ STEAMED	○ BROILED
○ CHAR-GRILLED	○ OTHER

SIDES	
○ FRENCH FRIES	○ ZUCCHINI FRIES
○ ONION RINGS	○ SWEET POTATO FRIES
○ SIDE SALAD	○ OTHER

NOTES

WOULD YOU GO BACK?		OVERALL RATING
○ YES	○ NO	/ 10

BURGER LOGBOOK

DATE	
BURGER JOINT	

LOCATION		COST	$

BURGER STYLE	

TOPPINGS		TYPE OF BEEF	
○ LETTUCE	○ ONION		
○ BACON	○ PICKLES	**TYPE OF BUN**	
○ TOMATO	○ CHEESE		
○ EGG	○ CHILI	**COOKED**	
○ AVOCADO	○ MUSHROOMS	○ PAN-FRIED	○ SMASHED BURGER
○ CHILES	○ OTHER	○ STEAMED	○ BROILED
CONDIMENTS		○ CHAR-GRILLED	○ OTHER
○ KETCHUP	○ MUSTARD	**SIDES**	
○ THOUSAND ISLAND	○ MAYONNAISE	○ FRENCH FRIES	○ ZUCCHINI FRIES
○ RANCH	○ RELISH	○ ONION RINGS	○ SWEET POTATO FRIES
○ BBQ SAUCE	○ OTHER	○ SIDE SALAD	○ OTHER

NOTES

WOULD YOU GO BACK?		OVERALL RATING
○ YES	○ NO	/ 10

BURGER LOGBOOK

DATE	
BURGER JOINT	
LOCATION	COST $
BURGER STYLE	

TOPPINGS

○ LETTUCE	○ ONION
○ BACON	○ PICKLES
○ TOMATO	○ CHEESE
○ EGG	○ CHILI
○ AVOCADO	○ MUSHROOMS
○ CHILES	○ OTHER

CONDIMENTS

○ KETCHUP	○ MUSTARD
○ THOUSAND ISLAND	○ MAYONNAISE
○ RANCH	○ RELISH
○ BBQ SAUCE	○ OTHER

TYPE OF BEEF

TYPE OF BUN

COOKED

○ PAN-FRIED	○ SMASHED BURGER
○ STEAMED	○ BROILED
○ CHAR-GRILLED	○ OTHER

SIDES

○ FRENCH FRIES	○ ZUCCHINI FRIES
○ ONION RINGS	○ SWEET POTATO FRIES
○ SIDE SALAD	○ OTHER

NOTES

WOULD YOU GO BACK?	OVERALL RATING
○ YES ○ NO	/ 10

BURGER LOGBOOK

DATE	
BURGER JOINT	
LOCATION	COST $
BURGER STYLE	

TOPPINGS

○ LETTUCE	○ ONION
○ BACON	○ P CKLES
○ TOMATO	○ CHEESE
○ EGG	○ CHILI
○ AVOCADO	○ MUSHROOMS
○ CHILES	○ OTHER

CONDIMENTS

○ KETCHUP	○ MUSTARD
○ THOUSAND ISLAND	○ MAYONNAISE
○ RANCH	○ RELISH
○ BBQ SAUCE	○ OTHER

TYPE OF BEEF

TYPE OF BUN

COOKED

○ PAN-FRIED	○ SMASHED BURGER
○ STEAMED	○ BROILED
○ CHAR-GRILLED	○ OTHER

SIDES

○ FRENCH FRIES	○ ZUCCHINI FRIES
○ ONION RINGS	○ SWEET POTATO FRIES
○ SIDE SALAD	○ OTHER

NOTES

WOULD YOU GO BACK?		OVERALL RATING
○ YES	○ NO	/ 10

BURGER LOGBOOK

DATE	
BURGER JOINT	
LOCATION	COST $
BURGER STYLE	

TOPPINGS

○ LETTUCE	○ ONION
○ BACON	○ PICKLES
○ TOMATO	○ CHEESE
○ EGG	○ CHILI
○ AVOCADO	○ MUSHROOMS
○ CHILES	○ OTHER

CONDIMENTS

○ KETCHUP	○ MUSTARD
○ THOUSAND ISLAND	○ MAYONNAISE
○ RANCH	○ RELISH
○ BBQ SAUCE	○ OTHER

TYPE OF BEEF

TYPE OF BUN

COOKED

○ PAN-FRIED	○ SMASHED BURGER
○ STEAMED	○ BROILED
○ CHAR-GRILLED	○ OTHER

SIDES

○ FRENCH FRIES	○ ZUCCHINI FRIES
○ ONION RINGS	○ SWEET POTATO FRIES
○ SIDE SALAD	○ OTHER

NOTES

WOULD YOU GO BACK?		OVERALL RATING
○ YES	○ NO	/ 10

BURGER LOGBOOK

DATE			
BURGER JOINT			
LOCATION		COST	$
BURGER STYLE			

TOPPINGS

○ LETTUCE	○ ONION
○ BACON	○ PICKLES
○ TOMATO	○ CHEESE
○ EGG	○ CHILI
○ AVOCADO	○ MUSHROOMS
○ CHILES	○ OTHER

CONDIMENTS

○ KETCHUP	○ MUSTARD
○ THOUSAND ISLAND	○ MAYONNAISE
○ RANCH	○ RELISH
○ BBQ SAUCE	○ OTHER

TYPE OF BEEF

TYPE OF BUN

COOKED

○ PAN-FRIED	○ SMASHED BURGER
○ STEAMED	○ BROILED
○ CHAR-GRILLED	○ OTHER

SIDES

○ FRENCH FRIES	○ ZUCCHINI FRIES
○ ONION RINGS	○ SWEET POTATO FRIES
○ SIDE SALAD	○ OTHER

NOTES

WOULD YOU GO BACK?		OVERALL RATING
○ YES	○ NO	/ 10

BURGER LOGBOOK

DATE			
BURGER JOINT			
LOCATION		COST	$
BURGER STYLE			

TOPPINGS

○ LETTUCE	○ ONION
○ BACON	○ PICKLES
○ TOMATO	○ CHEESE
○ EGG	○ CHILI
○ AVOCADO	○ MUSHROOMS
○ CHILES	○ OTHER

CONDIMENTS

○ KETCHUP	○ MUSTARD
○ THOUSAND ISLAND	○ MAYONNAISE
○ RANCH	○ RELISH
○ BBQ SAUCE	○ OTHER

TYPE OF BEEF

TYPE OF BUN

COOKED

○ PAN-FRIED	○ SMASHED BURGER
○ STEAMED	○ BROILED
○ CHAR-GRILLED	○ OTHER

SIDES

○ FRENCH FRIES	○ ZUCCHINI FRIES
○ ONION RINGS	○ SWEET POTATO FRIES
○ SIDE SALAD	○ OTHER

NOTES

WOULD YOU GO BACK?		OVERALL RATING
○ YES	○ NO	/ 10

BURGER LOGBOOK

DATE	
BURGER JOINT	
LOCATION	COST $
BURGER STYLE	

TOPPINGS

○ LETTUCE	○ ONION
○ BACON	○ PICKLES
○ TOMATO	○ CHEESE
○ EGG	○ CHILI
○ AVOCADO	○ MUSHROOMS
○ CHILES	○ OTHER

CONDIMENTS

○ KETCHUP	○ MUSTARD
○ THOUSAND ISLAND	○ MAYONNAISE
○ RANCH	○ RELISH
○ BBQ SAUCE	○ OTHER

TYPE OF BEEF

TYPE OF BUN

COOKED

○ PAN-FRIED	○ SMASHED BURGER
○ STEAMED	○ BROILED
○ CHAR-GRILLED	○ OTHER

SIDES

○ FRENCH FRIES	○ ZUCCHINI FRIES
○ ONION RINGS	○ SWEET POTATO FRIES
○ SIDE SALAD	○ OTHER

NOTES

WOULD YOU GO BACK?		OVERALL RATING
○ YES	○ NO	/ 10

BURGER LOGBOOK

DATE	
BURGER JOINT	
LOCATION	COST $
BURGER STYLE	

TOPPINGS

○ LETTUCE	○ ONION
○ BACON	○ PICKLES
○ TOMATO	○ CHEESE
○ EGG	○ CHILI
○ AVOCADO	○ MUSHROOMS
○ CHILES	○ OTHER

CONDIMENTS

○ KETCHUP	○ MUSTARD
○ THOUSAND ISLAND	○ MAYONNAISE
○ RANCH	○ RELISH
○ BBQ SAUCE	○ OTHER

TYPE OF BEEF

TYPE OF BUN

COOKED

○ PAN-FRIED	○ SMASHED BURGER
○ STEAMED	○ BROILED
○ CHAR-GRILLED	○ OTHER

SIDES

○ FRENCH FRIES	○ ZUCCHINI FRIES
○ ONION RINGS	○ SWEET POTATO FRIES
○ SIDE SALAD	○ OTHER

NOTES

WOULD YOU GO BACK?		OVERALL RATING
○ YES	○ NO	/ 10

BURGER LOGBOOK

DATE	
BURGER JOINT	
LOCATION	COST $
BURGER STYLE	

TOPPINGS

○ LETTUCE	○ ONION
○ BACON	○ PICKLES
○ TOMATO	○ CHEESE
○ EGG	○ CHILI
○ AVOCADO	○ MUSHROOMS
○ CHILES	○ OTHER

CONDIMENTS

○ KETCHUP	○ MUSTARD
○ THOUSAND ISLAND	○ MAYONNAISE
○ RANCH	○ RELISH
○ BBQ SAUCE	○ CTHER

TYPE OF BEEF

TYPE OF BUN

COOKED

○ PAN-FRIED	○ SMASHED BURGER
○ STEAMED	○ BROILED
○ CHAR-GRILLED	○ OTHER

SIDES

○ FRENCH FRIES	○ ZUCCHINI FRIES
○ ONION RINGS	○ SWEET POTATO FRIES
○ SIDE SALAD	○ OTHER

NOTES

WOULD YOU GO BACK?		OVERALL RATING
○ YES	○ NO	/ 10

BURGER LOGBOOK

DATE	
BURGER JOINT	

LOCATION		COST	$

BURGER STYLE	

TOPPINGS		TYPE OF BEEF

○ LETTUCE	○ ONION
○ BACON	○ PICKLES
○ TOMATO	○ CHEESE
○ EGG	○ CHILI
○ AVOCADO	○ MUSHROOMS
○ CHILES	○ OTHER

TYPE OF BUN

COOKED

○ PAN-FRIED	○ SMASHED BURGER
○ STEAMED	○ BROILED
○ CHAR-GRILLED	○ OTHER

CONDIMENTS

○ KETCHUP	○ MUSTARD
○ THOUSAND ISLAND	○ MAYONNAISE
○ RANCH	○ RELISH
○ BBQ SAUCE	○ OTHER

SIDES

○ FRENCH FRIES	○ ZUCCHINI FRIES
○ ONION RINGS	○ SWEET POTATO FRIES
○ SIDE SALAD	○ OTHER

NOTES

WOULD YOU GO BACK?		OVERALL RATING
○ YES	○ NO	/ 10

BURGER LOGBOOK

DATE			
BURGER JOINT			
LOCATION		COST	$
BURGER STYLE			

TOPPINGS

○ LETTUCE	○ ONION
○ BACON	○ PICKLES
○ TOMATO	○ CHEESE
○ EGG	○ CHILI
○ AVOCADO	○ MUSHROOMS
○ CHILES	○ OTHER

CONDIMENTS

○ KETCHUP	○ MUSTARD
○ THOUSAND ISLAND	○ MAYONNAISE
○ RANCH	○ RELISH
○ BBQ SAUCE	○ OTHER

TYPE OF BEEF

TYPE OF BUN

COOKED

○ PAN-FRIED	○ SMASHED BURGER
○ STEAMED	○ BROILED
○ CHAR-GRILLED	○ OTHER

SIDES

○ FRENCH FRIES	○ ZUCCHINI FRIES
○ ONION RINGS	○ SWEET POTATO FRIES
○ SIDE SALAD	○ OTHER

NOTES

WOULD YOU GO BACK?		OVERALL RATING
○ YES	○ NO	/ 10

BURGER LOGBOOK

DATE	
BURGER JOINT	
LOCATION	COST $
BURGER STYLE	

TOPPINGS		TYPE OF BEEF	
○ LETTUCE	○ ONION		
○ BACON	○ PICKLES	TYPE OF BUN	
○ TOMATO	○ CHEESE		
○ EGG	○ CHILI	COOKED	
○ AVOCADO	○ MUSHROOMS	○ PAN-FRIED	○ SMASHED BURGER
○ CHILES	○ OTHER	○ STEAMED	○ BROILED

CONDIMENTS			○ CHAR-GRILLED	○ OTHER
○ KETCHUP	○ MUSTARD		SIDES	
○ THOUSAND ISLAND	○ MAYONNAISE		○ FRENCH FRIES	○ ZUCCHINI FRIES
○ RANCH	○ RELISH		○ ONION RINGS	○ SWEET POTATO FRIES
○ BBQ SAUCE	○ OTHER		○ SIDE SALAD	○ OTHER

NOTES

WOULD YOU GO BACK?		OVERALL RATING
○ YES	○ NO	/ 10

BURGER LOGBOOK

DATE	
BURGER JOINT	
LOCATION	COST $
BURGER STYLE	

TOPPINGS

○ LETTUCE	○ ONION
○ BACON	○ PICKLES
○ TOMATO	○ CHEESE
○ EGG	○ CHILI
○ AVOCADO	○ MUSHROOMS
○ CHILES	○ OTHER

CONDIMENTS

○ KETCHUP	○ MUSTARD
○ THOUSAND ISLAND	○ MAYONNAISE
○ RANCH	○ RELISH
○ BBQ SAUCE	○ OTHER

TYPE OF BEEF

TYPE OF BUN

COOKED

○ PAN-FRIED	○ SMASHED BURGER
○ STEAMED	○ BROILED
○ CHAR-GRILLED	○ OTHER

SIDES

○ FRENCH FRIES	○ ZUCCHINI FRIES
○ ONION RINGS	○ SWEET POTATO FRIES
○ SIDE SALAD	○ OTHER

NOTES

WOULD YOU GO BACK?		OVERALL RATING
○ YES	○ NO	/ 10

BURGER LOGBOOK

DATE	
BURGER JOINT	
LOCATION	COST $
BURGER STYLE	

TOPPINGS

○ LETTUCE	○ ONION
○ BACON	○ PICKLES
○ TOMATO	○ CHEESE
○ EGG	○ CHILI
○ AVOCADO	○ MUSHROOMS
○ CHILES	○ OTHER

CONDIMENTS

○ KETCHUP	○ MUSTARD
○ THOUSAND ISLAND	○ MAYONNAISE
○ RANCH	○ RELISH
○ BBQ SAUCE	○ OTHER

TYPE OF BEEF

TYPE OF BUN

COOKED

○ PAN-FRIED	○ SMASHED BURGER
○ STEAMED	○ BROILED
○ CHAR-GRILLED	○ OTHER

SIDES

○ FRENCH FRIES	○ ZUCCHINI FRIES
○ ONION RINGS	○ SWEET POTATO FRIES
○ SIDE SALAD	○ OTHER

NOTES

WOULD YOU GO BACK?		OVERALL RATING
○ YES	○ NO	/ 10

BURGER LOGBOOK

DATE	
BURGER JOINT	
LOCATION	**COST** \$
BURGER STYLE	

TOPPINGS

○ LETTUCE	○ ONION
○ BACON	○ PICKLES
○ TOMATO	○ CHEESE
○ EGG	○ CHILI
○ AVOCADO	○ MUSHROOMS
○ CHILES	○ OTHER

CONDIMENTS

○ KETCHUP	○ MUSTARD
○ THOUSAND ISLAND	○ MAYONNAISE
○ RANCH	○ RELISH
○ BBQ SAUCE	○ OTHER

TYPE OF BEEF

TYPE OF BUN

COOKED

○ PAN-FRIED	○ SMASHED BURGER
○ STEAMED	○ BROILED
○ CHAR-GRILLED	○ OTHER

SIDES

○ FRENCH FRIES	○ ZUCCHINI FRIES
○ ONION RINGS	○ SWEET POTATO FRIES
○ SIDE SALAD	○ OTHER

NOTES

WOULD YOU GO BACK?		OVERALL RATING
○ YES	○ NO	/ 10

Printed in Great Britain
by Amazon